150 Psalms

A COLLECTION OF GOD BREATHED POETRY

Keshan Singh

Ark House Press
arkhousepress.com

Some names and identifying details have been changed to protect the privacy of individuals.

Cataloguing in Publication Data:
Title: 150 Psalms: A Collection of God Breathed poetry
ISBN: 978-1-7645620-4-1 (pbk)
Subjects: POE003000 POETRY / Subjects & Themes / Religious; POE023080 POETRY / Subjects & Themes / Motivational & Inspirational; REL012040 RELIGION / Christian Living / Inspirational.

Design by initiateagency.com

Dedications

I firstly honour Roma Waterman (Heartsong, VIC) who gave me the idea, lesson and inspiration for writing my own Psalms. Heartsong has been a great blessing and I am honoured to be a part of it.

I also want to bless Sandy Gray (Heartsong, VIC) for telling me to "write more!" Thank you for always having been so encouraging and supporting me.

Cathy (Heartsong, VIC), thank you for everything in kindness and much love to you as always! I appreciate that you have always been soft, consistent and encouraging to me. I feel mothered by you.

Chris and Sybil (VIC), I always feel at home with you both. My brother and sister.

Richard, Rob, Josh and Smiley Josh, Callum, Keith, Dave E (QLD): I think of our men's group and all of you daily. I miss you all so much. Till we are reunited again in Brissy.

Michael (Freedom Centre VIC), I will never forget how you made me feel welcome as the first point of contact on my first day at Freedom. I was afraid and nervous about church and you took me in. Thank you for your continued faithfulness.

Patrick (USA), I am who I am because of you. Words cannot express my gratefulness. Thank you for standing by me each day and helping me to become more like Him.

Neshan (QLD), I love you brother.

Alessandra (VIC), you have so much potential in the faith and I encourage you to keep seeking Him. You are doing so well. There is such a strong calling on your life for His purposes, which will come to pass. My heart will always be toward you. Stay tiny.

Ian and Heather (VIC), thank you for nurturing me in my early days and staying up to date with me.

Laura (VIC), thank you for always caring about my life and my walk in Christ. There will never be anyone like you. Your care and your heart is special and I honour your faithfulness despite your challenges. Your daughters are precious jewels in the earth and none shall be like them, now and forever.

Abhishek (SG), "till the end brother." I speak a blessing over your new family. May your little angel be all that she is called to be, favoured in the eyes of God and man.

Grandpa (Nana Ji), I hope you can see how much I have accomplished. I remember you all the time. Rest well.

Contents

Opening Prayer

Jesus of Nazareth,

My prayer is that each person who reads these psalms will come to know more of your character and nature as a good and loving God.

I pray that I have expressed you well to each person who flips these pages.

I pray that each one will learn to see you for who you are- the one who dwells in unapproachable light.

Moreover, I pray that each word will dictate their experience of love and help each person to be connected to you intimately, in a special way.

I pray that your will be done through this book.

Please trouble the hearts of those far away from you, coax them in your love and bring them home.

I seek the return of people far off, that those who are not your beloved will come to know you and become your beloved.

In you we live and move and have our being.

May it be unto us according to your will.

You are a shield about me, the glory and the lifter of my head.

In Your name,

Amen.

Keshan Singh

Introduction

Dear reader,

This book serves as a compilation of my expression of the Lord's glory through poetry. As you read each Psalm, which has been written by me through the influence of the Holy Spirit, you will see my heartfelt expression of God's ways and attributes, and the revelation of His loving character, through His Son Jesus

Some of these Psalms are written based on the journeys I have been on with the Lord, and my personal, enriching experiences with Him. Other Psalms are written based on the revelations given to me by the Holy Spirit.

I pray you find some comfort if you can relate. I pray your knowledge of Him grows intimately and increasingly in every way.

My hope is that they will enlighten your heart to the faithfulness of God despite all opposition, suffering and impossibility. It is important to grasp that His character does not change and will never change until the very end of time.

You may find that some of the Psalms may get repetitive, however my understanding of it is just a continuous reemphasis of His goodness, glory, majesty and love towards YOU.

These Psalms are what the Holy Spirit has given me, and nothing is of my own work. He has used my journey to shape what is recorded.

I pray each Psalm will bring you blessing and insight beyond measure, of how great, deep, far and powerful the love of God is for all who exist, especially for YOU.

Read this 10 times over and reflect on what God has said about you-

> ***"I'll show up and take care of you as I promised and bring you back home. I know what I'm doing. I have it all planned out—plans to take care of you, not abandon you, plans to give you the future you hope for. When you call on me, when you come and pray to me, I'll listen." – Jeremiah 2911-12 MSG***

Be hopeful in all things, He's right there waiting for your response.

Call Jesus.

See what happens.

Psalm 1

Your Glory light falls on my shoulders,
As your presence engulfs my being.
O' God you fill my life with hope and purpose, going before me into all areas of life.
Though I fall daily, your Hand carries and restores me to peace.
Lord, you hear my every cry and grief.
You rush quickly to envelope me in comfort.
My feet are planted firmly.
I see you as my fortress, repelling the waves of evil.
You are my strong tower.
Who can stand against you?
You are my shield and my companion through trials of sorrow.

Psalm 2

Although I turn my face from you oh God,
You remain steadfast in your promises towards me.
Your Words create a shelter over my life,
Ensuring safety and complimenting the desires of my heart.
Your unwavering love draws my face to turn towards you.
And therein I behold the essence of your Glory.
My cry goes before me to Your throne; yet you step down and meet my needs.
You write my life into the fabric of the world,
And cause it to flourish, bringing you the glory.
I feel the vibration of your beating heart,
And my spirit rings with heaven's frequency.
My entire being responds to the sounds of your footsteps,
As I look up and see my friend.
You are my destiny.

Psalm 3

As I bear witness to the endless stream of the waterfall,
I am reminded of your endless faithfulness to me.
Without beginning, without end.
Your face is timeless.
Your promises flow eternal,
Continuously streaming into all areas of my life.
The sound of your river rings true to my ears,
The rushing stream edifies me.
As I lean in to quench my thirst,
I find you quench my heart.
As I dip in, I experience your grace.
You cover me in peaceful promises.
You wash me clean as I am soaked in your presence.
I remain true to you as I find myself returning to your stream.
Your water is the only water that can keep me clean.
I see You dipping in with me,
I see You calling me into the deep.

Psalm 4

Oh Lord, there is no boundary line that can contain your love,
I cannot understand it.
Why do you pour out undeserving grace,
Despite my feeble attempts to please you?
I am nothing, yet to you I am everything.
Your love has cast out my wrongdoings,
Your love eviscerates all pain from me.
Who am I, that thou hast chosen me?
Does the servant set himself above the master?
Never, yet you dine with me in the confines of my heart.
Your love calls me friend.
You come to me and call to me each morning, before I can
    remember You.
Your love washes my feet, that I may tread upon a clean path.
I break, but you keep me upright.
Thou hast charged me to reveal Your undeserving love to the
    broken.
I will radiate Your good pleasure and show the way to Your heart.
I see Your salvation,
Which has come from love.

Psalm 5

As the enemy encircles me, numbering in the thousands,
I stand on His Word.
I prepare myself, ready to heed His commands.
His eyes are on me; His face is toward me.
He holds my right hand up with a spear,
He bears His shield upon my breast.
I am adorned with His garments.
I keep His face before me.
I fear not.
The enemy encloses on all sides.
Yet the Lord commands me to wait.
The enemy growls fiercely, yet I am not moved.
He counsels me to remain fixed on Him.
He proclaims: the battle is His.
His perfect light shines from above and the enemy flees in agony.
Behold, the Light of the world in His fierce glory.
I will keep my eyes upon His council.
Although prepared, I am not moved.
I have seen with my own gaze: the darkness flees the Light.
The Lord God fights for me.
The Holy One of Israel commands all: seen and unseen.

Psalm 6

In the early morning, I call Your Name.
I seek to connect with You.
Before I finish my words, I can sense You.
Right next to me, I feel You.
Your presence is apparent.
Your comfort is radiant.
I have seen You next to me.
Wherever I go, when I close my eyes,
I see You.
Lord, you follow me.
You have trained my mind to look for You.
I am dependant on Your peace.
I cannot part with You.
I look away and yet You are there.
Where are You not? You fill my space.
Each environment harbours Your presence.
I am kept at peace.
By the power of our connection, I walk in confidence.
My silver cord is tied to You,
Bound together for eternity.
I look only for You.

Psalm 

Lord Jesus, I see your Face.
Your crystal blue eyes reveal the depths of your love for me.
Your bright rosy cheeks mirror the apple's reflection.
Olive skin, perfectly tanned,
Luscious wavy hair till the back of your neck; shares the same tone,
As your perfectly trimmed beard of light brown.
Your face is brighter than any light I've seen,
Yet I can look into its details and find everything.
From Your image I can catch the waves of Your love; emanating.
All of creation responds to Your arrival.
The barren ground springs forth life.
The oceans waves are calmed and stilled.
The creatures speak forth Your praise.
The volcanoes are tamed whilst the rocks leap for joy.
The winds howl Your praises to the ends of the earth.
The planets vibrate and give forth their frequencies.
All that is seen and unseen responds to Your arrival
For we recognise You, Creator of all.
Your beauty is known until the boundaries of the end of Your Creation.
Is there any end to this?
I see You, so I can see the Father.
We are known to You.

Psalm 

Lord, I close my eyes and I am at Your presence.
Green lilac fields stretch for miles unto the horizon.
An endless number of angels decorate the skies in the firmament of heaven.
Their cries of praise echoes throughout the airwaves of heaven,
Showering believers in a rainfall of tangible praise and bliss.
Thrones upon thrones decorate the inner sanctum of the temple of His glory.
His temple is the centre of the kingdom.
The capital of glory from which the light of God shines,
and enlightens the entire heaven.
All believers who walk through the city streets of this celestial and eternal kingdom cannot hide from His light.
The colours of the rainbow, the evidence of His ancient promise,
interwoven in the winds of the air, soar throughout the city as a banner of His continuous love.
The monuments of the heroes decorate the corners,
For their good works are remembered before their God.
The streets are encrusted with majestic rubies, layered upon the finest gold
The highest peaks of heaven, harbour the angels of His,

Who stand watch over the safety of the saints; for who the Father
creates for according to their desires.
The satisfaction and the joy of the saints continuously expand;
there is no end to anything.
The aroma of the Father's love comes to life and embraces each
saint by the second.
All the saints gather around His throne, accompanied by the Elders.
The living beings and the angels take their place, as the Cherubim
proclaim His holiness throughout His perfect empire.
The saints are marched up towards the throne of the Son, with
whom He shares, for those who conquer.
The Word of God smiles and embraces each one,
As the Father looks upon with approval.
They are then taken to the Father, who loves each child individually
for 10,000 years.
All are filled with joy, as they sing praises to Him who has reunited
the lost,
To the one Lamb who holds the banner of victory.
There is no pain, there is no sorrow.
All are kept in Father's Arms, like there is no tomorrow.
Amen.

Psalm 9

As I speak forth praise, He manifests
His presence is alive; encapsulating my space
Where are my griefs? Where are my woes?
They have fled from me, as the Lord has come
The bearer of my shame, the One who cares for my life
Causes the darkness to flee and heralds holy light
I am overcome with joy and I leap for His glory
He has made Himself known to me.
I am rested upon Him as He holds me upright
He causes me to remember Him, despite the evil of this world.
How long more must we suffer evil? How long, O Lord, must we
    witness the terror which has overcome.
None of it has power in His sight; I must keep looking to Him.
As he walks in, all shame dissipates.
I am filled and my thirst is quenched.
He makes my being complete; I do not lack.
I understand that the One who has saved me has completed my
    inner being.
I make space for nothing else, but the joy of the One who gives vigour.
I am not laid to waste, all that I am is resurrected in His sight.
I will marvel at His Hand as He holds the world and everything in it
He is the depth of all understanding;
My fountain of wealth.
I will continue to invite Him in; as His aroma lingers,
longing for my partaking.

Psalm 10

He will not abandon me.
He will reward the work of my hands.
I have laboured tirelessly for Him and He will bring me
recompense.
Do not grow weary in doing good.
Opportunities will come for me.
My blessings will overtake me.
He continues to work in the background of my life,
Pulling all things for the benefit of my soul.
I do not see it, but I sense the change of pressing onward.
The Lord can be trusted, within pain and discomfort.
He trains my spiritual muscles to prepare me for times ahead.
He strengthens my resolve and enlarges my capacity.
He leads me where He needs me, and I enter into breakthrough
after breakthrough
I please Him in my growth.
I am becoming like His Son, Jesus.

Psalm 11

I walk through the wilderness of the country.
He meets me at each milestone, beckoning me onward.
I tire and I thirst.
He raises wells of living water, as I press forward through the heat.
He is making a smooth path ahead, under the Son.
As I trek, He breaks off former things of old.
Doors are preparing to be open, though I see no reprieve.
He teaches me to walk in freedom, where there is nothing holding me back.
He is my freedom.
He transitions me forward and demonstrates the method to liberty.
He is liberty.
I step through the first door, and many more are lined up for me.
These doors combine into one massive door,
Revealing to me I am yet to experience a massive outcome.
Big obedience brings me big outcomes.
He hearkens my ear to His voice,
That I may do only what He commands.
He is ultimately in charge over all.
The wilderness and the dry places bow to His river.

Psalm 12

Challenge after challenge,
I must learn to let go.
By His Hand all things fall into place and have their meaning.
I am accelerated into the path of blessings and opportunity.
Though my sight is limited,
It is up to Him to release all blessing over me.
He sees the beginning and the end.
His sight is unlimited, from Eden to the New Jerusalem.
How can I not trust Him?
My faith propels me, it secures me in Him.
I am never lost,
My saviour sees and finds me where I am.
He knows what He is doing.
He uproots and He plants.
He cares for me through all labour and toil.
When I am weak, He cares for my heart.
He handles me gently, and breathes into my soul.
He will remove all dread and death as He nourishes me
Why do you groan, O my soul?
Why do you doubt, careless mind?
Have you not seen His victory over your life?
Upon the high rock I am set, my feet are kept by His holy angel.
Victory is in my reach; He has won all things.
He becomes more and more faithful towards me.

Psalm 13

The Rock of Ages has been a blessing to me
He has provided me with overflow,
The cup of my blessing has been poured out
It flows down to other cups, which in turn flow upon others
There is endless grace available,
He has made me the head,
My gladness is brought into fruition.
He notices my works,
He sees when I rest.
His reward awaits me in the next realm.
Are you tired? Pray
Are you heavy in spirit? Rejoice
He trains me for international blessing.
He grooms me as His elect.
He crowns me with glory and makes everything effortless for me.

Psalm 14

How does one remain firm and steadfast?
They remain in the True Vine.
How does one draw strength when they are weak?
They plug into the nourishment of His presence
How does one come back to the place of promises?
They look for the sparkle of His glory.
How does one find their purpose and character?
They look upon the one who moulds.
How does one shine brighter by the day?
They are carefully refined in the furnace.
What man calls weak, God redeems and calls strong.
Without a second thought one must surrender,
There they will find all they need.
It is fitting for Him to elevate His servants,
And cause them to do the impossible.
One must simply be dressed in His armour,
Wait for His voice,
Know Him intimately,
And all they will experience is success and victory.

Psalm 15

He reveals His heart to me;
One that is filled with compassion and mercy
Though I am buried in my grief and troubles
The light of God reaches me where I am
It penetrates to my being and His voice calls me out of ailments and sorrow.
It is He who raises my head,
He shines His face towards me
He pulls me forward into His light and reveals His mercy and grace
He loves me upon His chest,
He reaffirms my identity.
I am who He says I am,
I have what He says I have
He enlightens my heart, that I may reflect His glory to the world.
He sets me in the midst of those who would bless me
I have friends who are in Him
They recognise my light,
He has built a community around me, and they know me intimately
I am surrounded with my soldiers, who would die for me
As Christ lives in them, they bear me up
I am a leader of this community, they honour me
Jesus is the head, so I am elevated.

Suffering is temporary, His rewards are forever
I am seen by Him.
Circumstances do not dictate my path
He calls me to conquer
And there He waits for me with a crown of glory
I am His and He is mine
Amen.

Psalm 16

Where the Lord leads,
He will guide, He will provide
He will guide you to the places He has called you to minister in
You will follow His voice, into the valleys and the mountains.
Remain faithful to His commands,
And surely, He will raise you to triumph
Bear the armour of the faith,
Adorn it as a general of His army.
Rise to the occasion,
Lead the 10,000
If he calls you, He will guide you, He will supply for you
You will never lack.
He equips you for every war,
For each victory, He esteems you with a ruler's rod
Crown after crown, the spoils belong to you.
For where He is, you will be also.
Do not doubt what He has said,
He is a God of His word, which shall remain forever
In your doubt, remember His character
Each and everything which He commenced in you,
Shall take its fruitful place and find its completion,
In your abundant life.

Psalm 

O God, I have fallen yet again,
My desires tempt me.
Though I remember your goodness from times past,
My desires haunt me
Time after time, you forgive me,
Yet I return to stain myself.
How much longer will my flesh overtake me?
Why do I do the things I keep doing?
Your Word promises cleansing towards me,
Yet I stumble as I keep walking.
You O Lord are holy and true,
Your faithfulness and compassion outweigh my disgrace
There are portions of mercy for each and every dirt
I will hold your mercy in a tight embrace
Lord I long for your cleansing touch,
Your blood covers my gravest sin
Nothing is too harsh; for you to turn your Face
No act is too unclean that you would desert me in filth
You see pathways for your goodness to shine,
Despite the fact I fall every time
I will continue to boast in how much you love me,
I stumble in filth and take many steps backward,
Yet in an instant, your lovingkindness propels me into glory and life.

Psalm 18

Man questions his purpose,
And strives to make a name for himself,
Does he know that all his efforts are in vain?
Foolish one, how long will you seek for that which is fleeting?
Why do you look for temporary gain?
Has not God breathed His life into your lungs?
Did he not set the mysteries of eternity into your heart?
Days go by as you strive to attain,
The same days are fleeting and running from you,
What have you really achieved?
Has not God prepared the end of all days?
Has He not already determined what abides forever?
So then why do you only look for what you see?
The Shepherd has promised a kingdom without end,
His Mind has envisioned what we cannot comprehend
We cannot describe the treasures which await us,
In a perfect union above the heavens
Why do you strive to make temporal name for yourself?
Generations will eventually forget.
His eyes are upon those who have eternity in mind,
Monuments are raised in the unseen realm, for those who die daily
to themselves.
Time is fleeting so choose what you will.
You will enter into eternity with nothing from this world.

Psalm 19

Jesus has called me upon the waters.
I have made my ark,
I have lifted the sails.
His boat carries me to deep waters.
I am in the open.,
Nothing or no one can be seen for miles.
His wind catches my sails,
I am rushing upon the waters.
Waves are created from my journey on all sides.
The whales surface and escort me.
The birds descend to feed me.
Clouds form and the roars of thunder echo.
Flashes of light illuminate the darkness.
I am alone, vulnerable from all sides.
There is no dent on the boat.
The waves carry me forward.
His holy angel appears to comfort me.
He has kept me safe in the bubble.
'Peace be still' echoes in the atmosphere.
The waves settle and calm overtakes the waves.
The sky clears and I see a light on the waters.
Behold, the Bright and Morning Star is walking towards me.

Psalm 20

Where the Lord has led me,
He has granted me grace and favour amongst mankind and in heaven.
He will lift me up before man,
That they all may behold the light of the Living Christ in me.
He has chosen me.
He is carving my path ahead to glory.
He is beckoning me forward to prosper me.
People will begin to recognise the Lord in me,
For I carry the wells of living water.
He leads me to the promise land where He seeks to plant me.
He uproots all that is not meant for me.
He promises my renown for the purpose of His ministry.
I submit to Him daily,
His authority rules every area of my life.
I must remain within His presence,
I endeavour to abide in His love.
He is the author of my faith,
I daily meditate on His mercy.
For all I have, my full and abundant life,
Is released through Him, and for Him.
The supplier of the hope of my calling.

Psalm 21

I am brought out from the world.
There is no one, or nothing around me.
I am caught up in a secret and enclosed cave.
The space where there is no noise from the world, nor interference.
I am at a point where it is just me and Him.
2 of us intertwined, His voice echoes in the quiet.
This is spiritual growth, in the closeness of His presence.
There is no one to address but Him, no can listen, but only Him.
I am brought into the deep, can I follow Him in?
My great Father, I am His son.
He takes me into the comfort of His arms.
There is no world around me, I am in the blackness of space.
He is my only light, He is the only sound I hear, the only One I experience.
He is my portion of great growth; I am learning to grow in Him.
He is preparing me for greater things, so He has hidden me.
All things are closely linked in Him,
The hiddenness serves it purpose.
He goes before me to open the doors of my blessing; I am yet to step out of transition.
He mentors me in maturity, my spiritual capacity is increased.
I resist and curse, yet He loves me, He knows my pain.

He stretches me, yet is closely watching me, attentive to my cries.
I will be the first to pioneer forward, post training and maturity.
He stretches me that others may see my suffering, and how He
redeems it.

Psalm 22

Where is the Lord? Where can He be found?
In the morning, I awake, I do not sense Him.
I search the early sky; I cannot feel Him.
I hunger and thirst for His love,
I cannot see Him.
Is the Creator hidden from me?
Does He loathe my sight, the stain of my sins?
Throughout the bustle of the day, I cannot hear Him.
I search for Him at every opportune moment,
Moment by moment I am in prayer, I call His name
Be not thou far from me, O God.
For in thy presence, you give light and hope.
Why does He speak so silently?
Why can I not hear Him
I long for the eruption of His presence,
The breakthrough of His delight.
My God has promised to never forsake me,
I trust He is closer than ever to me.
I trust His Word and His promise.
For He has set out to accomplish His will in my life.
He will love me till the very end,
I know He will make His face known.
Ah! There I see Him, He is present,
Within the inner confines of my spirit! Look inward.

Psalm 23

He is my leader and my guide.
My ultimate supplier; I have it all.
He permits me rest within the fields of plenty.
He walks, and calls me to walk beside the calm rivers
The inner strength of my heart.
I am trained for righteous living, to bring glory to His name.
Although I am caught in the dark paths of this evil world;
I am not ashamed of His presence.
I am brave; and I carry His authority and sword.
They remind me of who I am.
He brings me to an ultimate feast, near those who would take my life.
He pours His spirit over me and I am blessed beyond measure.
My joy is complete, and I am forgiven daily, forever.
I will remain within the confines of His Holy temple,
As I live in this life and the next.

Psalm 24

I have looked far and wide
To give meaning to myself
I have looked in vanity,
As I scouted the philosophies of the world
I have looked amongst companions and lovers,
Yet I am incomplete
I have looked at pagan practises,
Amongst the palms and stars,
Yet I am incomplete.
I have looked at idols, living and stone,
They provide false comforts and empty promises,
Yet I am incomplete.
I turned to the God of Israel in surrender,
I reasoned and wrestled with Him.
He pointed me to His word,
He spoke to my heart and spirit
He renewed my soul and being, He washed me clean.
He shared His secrets with me and repositioned my life,
Now I am complete.
He raised to life my identity and provided the hope of my calling.
Only He alone, the true Potter,
Has formed me and given me my meaning.

Psalm 25

My God is beautiful.
O' how the angels worship Him.
They have encircled Him for millions of years upon forever.
He is eternal, He has no beginning nor end.
The Cherubim and saints lay down before Him.
The company of prophets and elders throw themselves before His might.
He is magnified in all of Heaven,
Which shines His glory upon the earth.
The Son of God rules eternal, our Bright and Morning star, radiant with hope and love.
Who can withstand this measure of glory?
His light pierces all things created, seen and unseen.
His voice commands all of creation, to move and have its place.
The One who will subdue all things to Himself, calls me His friend.
How can one resist His splendour?
Can any man run from His majestic sight?
Even when one turns away, His command echoes in their being, He brings them home.
Your entire body responds and vibrates to His heavenly call.
Look to the cross, and discover the portal to eternity.
The open heavens are for you to reach,
O' broken man.

Psalm 26

I want to go be with the Lord Jesus.
I want to go to His peace.
I want to be near His feet.
I want to speak with Him
I desire His face above all.
I can only see a little on this earth.
He is very glorious,
He calls me upward.
He has promised a place for me.
He has been so faithful and true to me.
He has kept all His promises toward me.
I long for more of heaven and less of earth.
I want to feel His waves of abundant love.
I want to sit with Him in our secret garden.
Jesus, stay close to me.
I wish to meet all Your prophets and saints.
I want to touch the wounds on Your hands and feet.
I wait for the moment You call me home.
I must remain faithful to you here on earth.
For we have much to do together.
Show yourself to me here,
Give me hope and patience.
I want to be with Jesus.

Psalm 27

To walk away from Him is to abandon hope.
Where would I go?
To whom would I turn to?
What is left for me without His purposes?
Where is my vindication?
Shall I lay down my life now?
How can I go on without the sole provider of my hope?
If I abandon Him now, I am left to pursue my own desires.
This is vanity.
There is no meaning apart from Him.
Immediately there will be hopelessness.
It is a mistake for eternity.
How can I leave the one who holds my inheritance?
My desires may please me for a while,
But my heart desires what is eternal and everlasting.
He is the only eternal truth.
If I walked away, sooner or later pain will seep in,
Everything will make no sense,
My life would be void of meaning and joy.
The thrill of the flesh is temporary,
But the hopelessness will be forever.
I must not abandon Him at all costs.
Truly it is worse to walk away knowing Him than never having
known Him at all.

Psalm 28

O come and see the Lord,
See Him in the highest temple
O come and exalt the Lord
Bear witness to His glorious splendour
O let us bow,
In reverence and awe
For He holds the keys to life and death.
O come and bring our worship,
Lay it down at His heavenly altar
Let us walk in, into His holy of holies
Let us join hands with all who've gone before us
Let us make way for those who are to come
O come all ye, let us give thanks to the King
Seated high above all things seen and unseen
We have a special place, amongst His friends and servants
O come and see, be bold and examine
The purest light in the universe
O come and let us observe,
How He slays the evil one.
Let us behold,
How He tramples above all evil
Let us rejoice, for He has purchased our victory
Pass around the goblet of blessing,
Let us drink and be refreshed as we celebrate His living water.

Psalm 29

Who can anticipate the move of God?
He moves quickly, in mystery, within unimaginable fathoms.
He will cause the righteous and patient one to flourish amongst the thorns.
He cannot be contained to a mortal's comprehension.
He operates above all logical patterns and thinking.
He dwells outside the scope of human patterns.
He brings His people in unexpected places.
He causes the sun to rise on those who face Him in all circumstances.
Who can comprehend the mind of the living God?
Who has ever understood Him?
He blesses His faithful from glory to glory.
He opens the path and brings the increase.
He tells us what a thing is, and we marvel when He establishes it.
He brings all things together and authors our testimonies.
His people rejoice as He works behind the scenes.
He is a fruitful God, the tree of all livelihood.
Everything means something with Him, nothing is wasted in His kingdom.
He trains us to expect the impossible.
Don't fear, mortal man, only believe
We are His friends, how much more will He bring goodness to our hearts?

Psalm 30

The pathways are open in the fields.
I will not fall to the side.
Holy Spirit, take my hand and walk with me.
The path is set before my eyes.
His light leads my feet.
My faith keeps me moving forward.
I do not see the ultimate destination; I only see 2 steps ahead.
The saints follow me as I pave the way forward.
Many eyes are upon me as I lead in His example.
I will remain faithful to my God as I am led forward.
My enemies remain beside the path, seeking to veer me off.
My God continues to call me forward, despite temptation.
The opportunities over take me.
Disappointments bow before the path He has set me on.
If He has ordained my path, He will bring it to fulfillment.
No path is left unfinished in the Lord,
All righteousness is fulfilled in His name.
Creation groans to see His people revealed.
The earth cries out for restoration.
It is not yet for me to understand all things,
It is for me, however, to obey all His words and commands.
I will know what I need to know,
By His will,
In time, or in eternity.

Psalm 31

He teaches me to trust Him.
How can one's trust be fortified, unless they persevere through suffering.
He shares His secrets with me.
How can one know the deeper secrets, unless they are intimate with Him.
He states He will bring me across.
Where is my faith?
How can I go backward?
He leads me from all sides.
He trains my resilience to keep looking at His face.
He has an intricate plan for me.
He leads me one step at a time, sometimes two.
He has pushed away the filth, and brought me unto Himself.
He urges me to focus on that which is important.
He is the governor of my eternal perspective.
As I yield to Him, I understand what is worth living for and what is not.
I know what counts in eternity, and I strive accordingly.
He will not let go of my hand.
He secures me in Himself like a safety blanket.
I await the next step.

He causes things to happen quickly, as I obey Him.
I must wait in patience for His leading.
He has said He will come through for me.
If He has said it, He will do it.
He cannot deny Himself.

Psalm 32

Daily I lay myself down,
Daily I take up my cross.
Daily I do away with my selfish desires
Daily I partake in Your will.
Daily I exercise my faith in Your goodness
Daily I struggle with self-centeredness
Daily I learn to let go of what does not please you
Daily I resist temptation
Daily I battle with the lust of the flesh
I am vexed
It is a difficult battle
Daily I am set apart
Daily I walk in holiness,
Yet daily I fall also
Daily You encourage me,
Yet some days you remain silent
What way of life is this?
I am hard-pressed on all sides
I want to do what is right before you, yet my flesh beckons me to sin
Daily it is an internal struggle,
I have more than enough understanding of the spirit wanting to soar,
Yet the flesh is pulling me down
God, deliver me from the flesh, crucify my selfishness
Endow me with holiness, Lord, that I may be a pleasing sacrifice to You alone.

Psalm 33

There is a lighthouse on the horizon,
For all to gaze upon,
It burns brightly with blue fire
Upon all the land,
Those from far and wide,
Can see the beautiful glimmer
Those who are close,
Can feel the comforting warmth
This is the beacon upon a hill
For all to recognise and observe
They are drawn to this lighthouse,
There is light in the darkness!
This is how Elohim makes His people to be
Reflecting the light of His hope to the fallen world.
Amongst the darkest places, He sends His saints.
To light up and give hope to the atmosphere
Those who come and partake in the same hope
Are recreated into the same lighthouse,
Bearing His light and mark.
They are sent to make more amongst the darkness, until there is darkness no more
The multiplication of light drives out all pervading darkness
This is how He operates in the world.
Through the willingness of sacrificial saints, they are multiplied amongst men.

Psalm 34

I beheld a vision of myself,
Pouring out water which is alive from a drinking jug,
Into a large manmade hole.
It was waist high in height, assembled in a circular fashion by bricks.
The Lord set me before those in need,
As I poured out His water into the well.
The multitudes assembled and rushed towards the water.
It replenished their souls
They collected as much as they could and were engulfed with joy
and freedom
The water from a simple jug filled up the entire well,
And it overflowed!
God is a God of miracles, which disturb the human understanding.
Living water flowed everywhere,
People had more than they needed.
The Lord commanded not to move from that place,
All needed to have their thirst satisfied.
Respond to Jesus, and you shall never thirst again,
Truly a Kairos moment.

Psalm 35

Based on His majesty,
I bow my knees before the Father of Jesus our Lord,
Who has named and purposed all beings in heaven and earth.
That by trusting in Him,
We have access to the storehouse of His mercy and riches.
He grants us the strength we need daily,
Through the sovereignty of His spirit and access
He ministers to our inner man,
Therefore, allowing the person of Jesus to rise up in our hearts,
By our faith.
We shall establish our roots in the garden of His love,
That we may intimately experience the everlasting love,
The great measure of His lovingkindness,
And His loving sacrifice.
This love cannot be contained to the understanding of man,
It overflows amongst us.
It causes us to be filled within and made complete,
That we may be satisfied within ourselves, in Him.
I glorify the Chief of heaven,
Who is able to meet every need of mankind, and more than man
could ask for.
We bear witness to His works and powers thereof,
That He will be elevated as supreme over the church,
And give us the witness of His eternal Son, Jesus our Lord.
In this generation, and all the ones to come; until time eternal.

Psalm 36

Hear what the Lord has to say for the church.
His body, in one accord, is to be refined as gold.
The sifting is carried out, to separate the pure from the impure.
The Lord is looking for those who would endure,
Time and time again, the Body is tempted and has lost its way
It has lost the foundational value, which Christ initiated,
And purpose for the Body to fulfill.
There are those who seek to grieve amongst it,
There are those who seek to use it,
Where are those who would lay down their lives for it?
Where are those would give back into it
Commitments are without true expressions of faith.
The Lord is looking for those who would endure and remain faithful,
Whilst everyone else walks away.
The one who is faithful will be blessed, and the Lord will expand
    the Body upon his life.
The angels are looking for those who would serve the Body in all
    parts and areas,
They are looking to partner with these surrendered souls,
That they may be elevated and see God's restoration and manifest glory.
Who would stand in gap for his brother?
Who would put her hand up for her sister?

Where are initial family values which had intended from the
beginning.
Do not lose it amongst the culture of deceit.
Be not of the world, O Body.
See to it that you are restored to the Father.
He is looking for the melted hearts, not those who would resist.
He is looking for the surrendered ones,
Who would live their life fully on His Word and His commands.
The Body needs an elevation,
An upgrade is due.
The Father needs the willing members to bring the lost sheep into
alignment.
How else can the Body be strengthened to endure what is to come?

Psalm 37

Lord, it is Your promises which have blessed me,
Your faithfulness has kept me
You remind me daily of what is to come
You seek to give me more than I ask.
You seek to strengthen me to carry on
Your reminders are like fresh water splashed onto a dry soul
You are a faithful God
You keep Your promises to the letter
Despite setbacks,
You use failures to remind me how merciful You are.
You draw me close again and set my feet back onto Your path.
You walk in the closest proximity of my soul,
And remind me of the goodness of Your covenants.
You seek that which benefits my life, and that which is for me,
Never against me.
You set my past under Your covering, and paint me a new future.
One with Your hope and Your reward.
Time and time again, You have been faithful,
You bring my soul to the position You seek.
There You reward me with what You have promised me, and then more.
This is the truth from Abraham; You keep your covenants.
And I will declare that You O God;
You will finish what you have started

Psalm 38

Would I prefer to be accepted by man?
Or approved by God?
Am I living to please man?
Or do I pursue bringing glory to His name?
One cannot serve two masters.
He has no capacity for both.
He ought to choose.
Would he serve the one who is corrupt?
Or would he work for the One who is Perfect, the just One.
It matters not what man says, matters not what they suggest.
For when God has provided instruction, surely, He will test the heart of man.
He tests to see if they would remain true to Him,
Or if they would veer off His path to please people whom they know not.
Why would you please those who would soon forget your name?
They leave you temporary praise and move on to what is greater than you.
God has etched you into the palm of His hand,
He has remembered you before you were born,
And after you die, He will build a monument for you
In a place which has no end.

Mankind may erect a statue of stone, bearing your resemblance
It will wash away one day.
Chose whom ye will serve, be directed by the perfect and graceful One.
I implore you
He has prepared a place for you, which no man can prepare; one without end.

Psalm 39

I am the Lord's arrow.
The one whom He fashions daily.
He has specifically designed me and to be shot into the darkness,
To bring forth the light.
I am His weapon,
A specially crafted point,
For a specially ordained purpose.
I am special in His sight and one of a kind.
He handles His arrows with care,
But He tends especially to my sharpness.
The Lord God hath made my mouth like a sharp sword,
To declare His word to the generations.
He has hidden me within the shadow of His brilliant Hand,
And polished me as a mighty arrow.
I am formed to be the sharpest arrow of the quiver.
I am prepared to pierce the darkest shadows of the night,
To bring forth the light of the heart of Christ.
He has made me brave and strong,
As He draws me carefully and holds me in place.
He carefully aims upon the target which He has determined before time began.
He holds me in place upon the bow,

He waits for the perfect timing to shoot me forth.
The time comes and I am propelled, I speed forward quicker than light.
His arrow reaches His target, not veering one degree off sight.

Psalm 40

Who am I whom He has lifted up?
He has made me significant.
He has given favour to me.
He makes me stand out.
He calls me special amongst others.
How He has favoured me,
I cannot comprehend.
He makes me a blessing to different groups and peoples.
He makes them to bless me also.
He has opened doors of favour.
A man separated unto God,
Finds himself in a special position.
A place which others desire to be a part of.
The Lord is full of grace and favour.
He calls forward special ones and raises them for His great works
prepared before time.
He ordains all our help and assistance.
He honours the obedience and sacrifice of the one who has
struggled, yet is faithful.
My cup is overrun with favour.
My spirit is full of joy.
I cannot fathom the goodness and hope He has called me to.

Psalm 41

I will rejoice in His goodness.
I bow my head in thanksgiving.
He redeems all things.
He liberates me from suffering and despair.
He walks with me closely, day by day.
He enriches my life with wholesome experiences.
He promises a thing and fulfills it.
The lifter up of my head.
The One who saves and gives my meaning.
He is my rearguard.
Peace is my portion.
He has so much in store for me.
He gives me more than I expect.
I see His kindness everywhere
There is nothing He has not touched,
There is total freedom.
He blesses and blesses my life continuously.
His joy overtakes my life,
I cannot run from it.
His grace and mercy are unlimited.
He continues to love me in my shortcomings.
He is good to all mankind.

Psalm 42

When do we wrestle?
When do we surrender?
Does He not bring all things in His own time?
Do we frustrate ourselves in the wrong seasons?
Do we wait patiently through our testings?
When do we inherit what is ours?
We claim His promises,
But do we believe them?
We look upon His word,
But do we digest it?
How much faith are we willing to exercise?
God brings all things together in His beautiful time.
Position yourself daily and anticipate His arrival.
Seek Him first, not the promise.
Love who he is, no what is in His hand.
He is all things; he is all your promises.
Wrestle with Him and surrender after.
Declare His will daily and they will manifest.
Declare Him over all situations.
Be angry but be honest with Him.
Tell Him what aches you.
The God of peace will comfort you.
You will see the fullness of His promises and so much more.

Psalm 43

For one to lead, he must be tried.
For a man to have authority,
He ought to surrender first.
He is promised a reign on the mountains,
But he must walk through the valleys.
In the harsh terrain, he must first be shaped.
He must be moulded in the shape of the perfect One.
He must be trained in righteousness.
He must learn from the elders.
To lead, one must understand tough situations.
He must overcome hardship and rigorous battles.
He must speak from experience.
Should he submit and learn from others,
He will grow upright.
His head shall be above the clouds.
The Lord prunes the leader and fixes his roots in Him.
His capacity in enlarged, his patience in developed.
Man must wait on God's timing.
Man ought to remember that only God has prepared good works,
For him to walk in, through Jesus Christ,
Who is his Rearguard, Leader and Overlord.
You could be the worst, but He can make you the best.

All of your life is in His hands, give Him your heart.
That's what He is waiting for.
You can give it all to Him today.
Christ exchanged all of heaven's riches for your life.
He would do it all over again to have you, safe in His kingdom and arms.
You are what He desires.
You don't need to perish.
Please come to Him. Don't put it off.
You're not promised tomorrow.
I weep for you until you return to Him.
You were made to know Him.
You will find your purpose in Him for this life.

Psalm 44

He has graced me with recognition amongst the saints.
He has declared the year of favour.
He ordains people to walk alongside me for my development.
They take notice of my giftings.
He raises me up in different arenas,
He blesses my obedience.
Grace and favour are my portions.
In His flow, things are simple and easy,
They are not burdensome but light.
The blessings come to find me.
He has given me honour amongst men.
My roots are deeply established in Christ.
He appoints divine connections and raises up my community.
Treading the difficult path has amassed my rewards into fruition.
He has exceedingly abundantly more for me.
His anointing radiates upon my spirit.
His holy countenance is mine.
He equips me with keys to different treasures within people and
places,
That I may raise them up for His army.

Psalm 45

It is not possible to comprehend His grace and mercy.
It is out of this world to understand His willingness to be merciful.
Though we walk in the filth of the world,
He does not abandon us there.
He is very present,
He walks with us.
Though we resist Him, He follows closely behind.
Though we give into our flesh,
Submerging ourselves in our evil desires,
He does not turn from us.
How can this be?
"Depart from me Lord, I am sinful man."
Yet He remains. He is steadfast in loving and nurturing you through your faults.
His grace and mercy bring us back into divine restoration.
It is incredible to behold His love.
All He is, is love. Grace and mercy are what He is made of; unconceivable love.
He is willing to receive and restore the most evil of mankind.
He is seeking to restore those who are lost in the world.
Those who have gone astray and entertained false gods.
Those who have corrupted their bodies for gain.

He is looking for complete restoration.
Even those who know the truth, and fall on purpose or accident,
His grace and mercy meet them at every corner;
An unconceivable love.

Psalm 46

He dives in headfirst for your forgiveness.
He doesn't think twice,
He is always waiting,
Readily available to forgive and clean.
There is no description,
For how clean He can make you.
He cleans you perfectly in His blood.
It washes even the filth within the filth
Limitless depths of pure cleansing.
He does it quickly, instantly
And you can breathe in a new breath.
You feel a new thing.
The burdens are gone.
Your shoulders are light and you can stand upright.
His cleaning makes you endure his life
He cleans all those who come to Him
He cleans and cleans
He dresses and redresses the one who falls many times
He pursues you with forgiveness in mind
He redeems you quicker than you breathe in,
He does not hesitate.
So just come and be cleansed.
No psalm can describe this amazing redemptive feeling and power.

Psalm 47

Above all things, I put Him first.
He is the only source,
Who has made completion my norm.
Above all gifts, rewards and treasures,
I behold His glory.
This is His show, I am carried along the journey.
He brings me through beautiful and wholesome experiences.
I behold Him as the author of my story.
He knows how to bless me.
He knows what makes me happy.
He enlightens my heart.
There is so much being assembled around me.
I cannot keep up with His blessing.
How great and marvellous He is.
He has blessed my relationships and connections.
I cast my crown and robe before Him.
I consider all things loss,
That I may gain only Him.
All things are made for His love,
We breathe for His glory.
We fall in love with His love.

Psalm 48

The arm of the Lord,
It stretches across the globe,
Overshadowing the inhabitants.
How big this God is.
His arm is the carrier of all troubles and burdens.
His arm brings comfort and safety,
As he wraps it around His beloved.
The arm of the Lord is mighty.
It causes victory for the faithful few,
Over the hordes of evil.
His arm cleans up all principalities and strongholds.
With a swift sweep, He clears the sky.
He breaks it open.
He destroys the atmosphere of evil.
His arm changes the tides of battles and wars.
His arm saves us from the fires.
He reaches down to pull us up,
Upward towards our high calling in Him.
His arm holds the victorious spear,
Which pierces leviathan and sends it back to the deep.
His arm is our protective barrier,
The waters cannot overwhelm us.
His arm holds the universe.

Psalm 49

Grace is my best friend.
Grace covers me in a clean blanket.
Grace picks me up when I fall over.
Grace doesn't judge me.
Grace looks after my problems.
Grace pursues me relentlessly.
Grace chooses me.
Grace accepts me.
Grace invites me to commune with Him.
Grace removes all guilt and shame.
Grace brings me a new life.
Grace breathes freshness upon me.
Grace gives me strength for tasks.
Grace humbles me.
Grace trains me for challenges.
Grace adds blessing to me.
Grace revitalises my spirit.
Grace is always smiling at me.
Grace is holding me in His arms.
Grace will never judge nor condemn me.
Grace will lead me to His Father's house and keep me.
Grace is Jesus.

Psalm 50

We carry the Word of God in our heart.
We are the spiritual messages of faith to the fallen world.
We have imprinted the Good News into our spirits.
The very essence of Christ has been breathed upon us.
We are His living letters, with the cross as our letterhead.
His blood is our seal, His image our stamp.
We reflect His image to the world.
Line by line, word by word.
He is within our hearts.
How much greater is the ministry of our spirit?
We hold the permanency of His glory,
That we may reflect the eternal hope in our conduct and being.
We show people that the veil is removed,
We meet our God face to face.
Like Moses, they can have this too.
Bring them along, show them His glory, help them up the mountain.
The spirit is alive and active,
Carrying our living words to the hearts of our worldly friends.
They can have our message too.

Psalm 51

Our voices are trumpets.
With His power and authority manifest,
We echo His good hope to the nations.
He has commissioned and equipped us.
He trains our hearts and prepares our minds.
Our spirit is strengthened only in Him.
He leads us to grow and brings us deeper in Him.
This is so, that we may carry His sword to the nations.
Our voices are shaped by Him.
We release His frequency.
So, get up and declare His word to the nations.
Call forth the new generations to stand.
March out, blow the trumpets and declare His victory.
He orders our steps and prospers us in His ways.
He establishes us in our commissioning.
He reveals the next steps.
His Spirit goes before us and beckons us forward.
Let us go out to the harvest across the nations,
Let His angels carry us.
Let us be the labourers this world needs.
Bring unto the kingdom more co-heirs for His name's sake.

Psalm 52

The Lord tests those whom He chooses.
He brings them through a training so rigorous yet rewarding.
He brings them into the deep end where they sink or walk on water.
There are seasons of testing, and maturity of the faith.
A man can be afflicted with all things, but the Lord keeps Him.
The Lord shows Him the mature method of endurance.
He trains our capacity to endure that we may be faithful to the end.
How can a man, untested, endure the challenges of a greater walk?
How can a man, untested, develop character as an example to the world?
The Lord works every part of their minds and hearts.
He prunes and casts out all that is of no use for the next stage.
The Lord refines and controls the heat of the fire.
Though man falls during the testing, the Lord is gracious.
You will not fail during a test as long as you remain faithful to Him.
He carries all failure and burden during the endurance and walks in the fire with you.
He fans the flames of all the gifts and treasures of one's heart; they are revealed.
You begin to discover so much more of yourself.
The Lord has placed many treasure chests in you and they are opened through pain.

Multiple dynamics and dimensions of your inner man are
awakened,
To bring forth the giftings and anointings of God, on display upon
your head.
Be tested and prevail for your upward call.

Psalm 53

I rejoice in the Lord.
He has given me more than I can handle.
My blessings have overcome me, I struggle to keep up with His goodness.
He has given me an inheritance, worth more than anything imagined.
He has placed in my hand the abundance of eternal life.
He is storing up treasures for me in unseen realms.
I cannot begin to envision the glorious treats in store for me.
My heart is full.
He permits me to walk in His abundance.
The kingdom of heaven has more than enough,
I have full access to the abundance of His store house.
I reach up and pull down what I need,
That my joy may be complete.
I see all of my needs being met; nothing is left out.
I see an overflow in what He has given me.
I count greater the blessings of what I walk in, the connections I have made,
Rather than worldly possessions.
I have so much to give out now,
blessing has followed me as I have stepped out.

The Lord can be trusted to provide,
In any circumstance He will show His sovereignty over the
impossible.
He is the richest, and we have His riches.
Christ has prepared an inheritance for us to share in.
I will rejoice in the Lord, my sole provider.

Psalm 54

The prophet is called to a high order of kingdom service
The prophet harkens his ear to the voice of God,
Daily and nightly, he must meditate and receive from the mouth of God
The prophet may feel alone a lot of times,
For there are those who cannot connect nor understand
But the prophet must persevere during the cave seasons,
For God will groom his light to shine brighter than others,
When the time has come for him to be revealed.
The prophet is called to a high mountain top,
Where others cannot reach.
The trek is filled with obstacles and calamities,
This is where he must discern the voice of God,
He must completely abandon all he thinks he knows,
He must strip away and put to death his own desires,
And fall into the Hands of God for him to reach success and abundance.
The prophet must speak without fear wherever he is called,
Surely, he will be persecuted and hunted, he will flee,
But the Lord of Hosts will be there to restore and protect.
The prophet has greater authority than he thinks,
He is able to call heaven down and release abundance,

He can also decree the judgments of God.
The prophet is not to be taken lightly nor underestimated.
The ones who receive him share in all that he has accumulated for himself.
The prophet is very special.

Psalm 55

How great are my riches,
That I possess everything in Him.
In this I am comforted,
That I will not lack when I have Him.
I get to rely on Him and trust in Him.
I never have to doubt nor worry.
Despair brings me closer to Him,
That I may behold your glorious nature.
When I take my daily bread, I am filled.
In my body, soul and spirit I lack nothing.
We are fully sufficient in Him.
All that we suffer from prepares us for greater heavenly treasure.
We look to the unseen.
His spirit is our guarantee for our heavenly dwelling.
Let us remain clean and filled with thanks.
Our Redeemer has filled our lives with riches beyond comprehension.
He has overflowed my life with goodness.
I have more provision that I need.
I live from heaven's economy and stature,
Therefore, I am triumphant in this world.

Psalm 56

The Lord is the opener of all doors.
I sit and wait in delight.
He commands me to wait and observe.
He has been very true to His word.
Let go and let God, He is ultimately in control.
He has come through so much more than I could ever ask for.
He has shown me the worth of my troubles and blessed it in
multiplication.
I remember Him first over my woes.
I wait in patience and pray continually.
I sit still and remember the His goodness.
Hr brings everything in His timing.
He surprises me with His blessings.
Blessed is the man who waits on the Lord.
The Lord exhibits His full control over all situations.
He moves in the favour of His chosen.
He will not let His own fall.
He goes after His sheep and returns them to His fold.
He works to redeem the world through His own.
He is faithful.

Psalm 57

My Rock and Redeemer,
You have qualified and ordained me.
It matters not what man says.
I will exalt you above the heavens.
I throw up my praises to the stars.
My friend and King, would you catch them for me?
Oh, how you delight me.
You complete me in every measure
You give meaning to my suffering and justify it.
How abundant you are; filled with eternity.
I cannot begin to describe You, oh God.
Anointed One, would you rain heaven's glory upon my life.
I want to be covered in your light.
I want to shine like the stars.
I want to see Your glory.
You are sovereign over all things, seen and unseen, created and yet
to come.
The One who is able to subject and subdue all things to Himself has
become my greatest friend.
Thank you, Perfect One.

Psalm 58

He has shaped us for His plans and purposes.
Each one of us has been carefully moulded and crafted.
This is a beautiful journey;
That we are here to discover our purposes in Him
He has specifically selected our season of birth.
He has predestined our ministries before the foundation of the world.
He has called us out of filth in unique ways.
He has awoken the desires of our heart for His kingdom.
The light of God has awoken and filled us to completion
He has made us sufficient in every way that we may abound in good works.
He has desired that we should depend on and serve one another, as a collective.
He teaches us how to be, then, how to do for Him.
He works on our hearts and cleans it up.
He brings us through an evolution of character; to be like Jesus.
When we are amongst others, Jesus may be seen and glorified in you and me.
He teaches us to use our gifts, and depend on others for their gifts.
We are different and so unique, but serve the same Master.
He is Lord over all, and we contribute to His story for the earth.

We all have our place, our assigned designations.
We all have our crowds, the specific people groups to minister to.
We all have our special inner circle, who are there to encourage us forward.
We all have our same Lord, who shepherds us through this journey.
What a beautiful life, He has ordained.

Psalm 59

Hurts can happen without warning,
We praise the Lord regardless.
Afflictions take over and result in heartache
We praise the Lord regardless.
Doubt creeps in and make us question our foundations,
We praise the Lord regardless.
Hopelessness kicks in and we despair.
We praise the Lord regardless.
Blessed is the Most High King, who reigns supreme over all.
He has put everything under His and our feet.
We praise the Lord regardless.
Heartaches and betrayal can cause us to spiral
We praise the Lord regardless.
Persecution and mockery haunt our ears.
We praise the Lord regardless.
We are thrown to the pit or the prison,
We are cast out and ridiculed by man
We praise the Lord regardless.
He is the one who redeems the suffering servant.
He gives meaning to all pain and affliction.
He justifies our walk and brings us back into balance.
He is supreme and permits suffering for our growth and refinement.
He rewards the one who is faithful and endures to the end
I praise the Most High God, regardless.

Psalm 

He has come to give us life in abundance.
To expand the perimeters of our tent,
To bless our growth and prosper us in His Law.
His faithfulness knows no bounds,
He is the keeper of our hearts.
He is the caregiver of our souls.
He is the joy of our lives,
He blesses those who faithfully seek and abide in Him
Our tents are held down by our ropes when it is windy,
Allow His wind to blow your tent and stretch it far and wide.
For this purpose, He seeks to bless and expand your influence.
He is the Lord of all hope,
He is strong, mighty and powerful in all things.
He is our faithful deliverer and guardian.
He is the beginning and the end of all creation,
So would you trust Him to expand and grow you.
Though pain may set in for now, glory overcomes it forever.
Abide in Him as mature sons and allow the Father to carve His heart into you.
You are His chosen; the living tent of His presence.
He seeks to place His tabernacle in you.
That all man may look upon thee,
And bear witness to the face of the living Christ.
For whom do you seek to bless,
That you may bless them towards the Lord eternal.

Psalm 

Prepare your buckets, gather as many as you can.
The Lord is assembling the heavenly clouds over the land.
The prophets have called forth His heaven,
Assemble all ye broken,
Assemble all yea poor,
Bring the blind, carry the lame, retrieve the orphans and old.
The rain cometh!
It pours tremendously, it will flood the streets.
The windows of heaven have opened and the Lord has commanded His rain.
The prophetic flooding has commenced, it will overflow through the streets, into the rest of the nation.
Rivers will form upon the roads and no man will contain it.
More and more rain is called forth by the prophets.
The Lord is releasing as much as His faithful desire, and even more!
The enemies of the Lord flee from the flooding, they are numerous and they run for the hills.
The well of the land will never run dry.
His nation shall accumulate an abundance,
Other nations will take notice and come to the land of fruitfulness.
Be greatly fine tuned to the voice of the Lord, harken your ears to Him.

Declare of His overflow to the lands beyond the mountains, the
lands beyond the seas.
There is more and one nation cannot contain it.
Oh, how glorious is the Lord and His rain.
Heaven cannot be contained on the earth, for it is ever expanding!

Psalm 62

He has made me His dwelling place,
A living host of His immaculate presence
He chooses the most broken of vessels
To raise up as a display of His sovereignty.
He has designed me as a beautiful artwork,
Very special and extraordinary amongst the trillions
Jesus made friends with the outcasts and unlikeable,
He has so much time for you no matter what you think.
He will carve you carefully like a marble statue,
And present you as His beautiful work before the Father.
He desires to host Himself in the confines of your heart.
Therefore, open your inner sanctuary to experience His fullness.
He longs to overflow your cup with joy.
He wants you more than you think.
He rejoices over you for no reason, other than love.
He seeks to clothe you in His splendour,
That you may experience His heaven on earth.
I remember the promises of God daily;
They encourage me and keep moving forward,
Through the burdens, the struggles and barriers,
I continue to overcome and walk in victory daily.
He is making me His beautiful masterpiece,
The struggles and pain are added to His masterpiece
Because He makes beauty out of ashes.

Psalm 63

How sweet are Your words Oh Lord,
They are like honey to my soul
They nourish my inner man, and make my belly full
How amazing to serve in Your presence,
It fulfills my purpose and gives me assurance of identity.
You Oh God are precious to me;
You are the sovereign one
You allot each man unique abilities,
You bring individuals together with various skillsets.
You ordain a collective to serve and to build the kingdom.
You arrest the hearts of Your chosen and convict them to serve the poor.
Our gifts and abilities come only from You,
And you train us to develop and awaken many giftings inside of us,
That we may be used mightily to serve those in the world and the Body.
Only in you God do we find our reason to live,
Our reason to move forward and develop ourselves
You are the best character and professional developer.
You permit us to operate in unique spheres,
Where we find our special callings;
Therefore, we move upward and forward,

Running the race You have set before us to discover You and
ourselves.
To know ourselves, we must first know You
To know where we ought to stand, move to, and serve in
We are first called and ordained by You, Master.

Psalm 

The seed is planted by one within the ground,
The seed is watered by another within the ground.
It is the Lord who causes it to grow.
It bears much fruit and is tended to by one whom the Lord entrusts
it to.
In some grounds, the seed fights its way up to grow.
It has to contend with various factors
The ground may no longer be fertile.
However, the good Gardener is in charge over all elements.
He acts in miracles which defy all universal laws.
He brings the essence of heaven to that seed;
So much so that it shoots up even through concrete.
Something not possible has happened,
So, it will be with the righteous ones who believe.
He calls it to grow upward, not to the side or downward.
So long as the roots are found in Him,
It can grow through any circumstance.
It bears so much fruit that it attracts others.
It continues to be watered till it towers above others.
How can one grow in a manner as such?
To be connected to the heart of the Father causes a divine rising.
All are called to rise above circumstances, yet few do.
Where are their roots in? What is their nutrient?
Have they not given access to the Great Gardener to give nutrients
and trimming?

Psalm 65

You are the source of all goodness and peace.
My secret place, how comfortable You are.
I soak in Your love daily and open my heart to Your warmth.
Your gaze calms me in any situation.
I am at peace in Your mercy.
Your grace washes over me like the fresh wind on a hot day.
The breeze of Your essence relaxes me.
I see You everywhere,
Amongst the stars, the animals, the oceans, the clouds and forests.
I see Your clearly in my heart.
I can never ignore You, how could I ever turn my face from You?
You catch my eyes with unique signs and wonders.
My first love, how I adore You.
My spirit leaps for joy when I long for You.
Come hold my hand, Lord.
I seek to walk hand in hand with you.
Look into my eyes and comfort me, Perfect One.
Empower me to finish this life.
Stay close to me, my Chief.
Whisper to me the joys of heaven which await me.

Psalm 66

Through the growth,
Through the droughts,
I will trust in You, Lord.
I will praise Your name.
Lord, You are faithful.
It is not for me to doubt but to trust.
No matter what happens, I will love You first.
You have planned everything out for my life perfectly.
You know what will shape me and grow me.
Though it seems the wells are dry,
And the fields are littered with death,
I will drink of the Living Water, eternal and pure.
It refreshes my soul and gives me strength.
I will remain in shalom peace,
As I wait for my God to move for me.
There is much more for my life,
As I live and breathe, I serve His purposes.
I am kept safe in Him.
For He is my purity, righteousness and reward.
I will look into the unseen and reflect on the move of Your Spirit.
I will remember Your goodness and boast of it all the more.
You are my first and last.

Psalm 67

You are so beautiful, Lord.
You are so perfectly pure.
I love You so very much.
I cannot take my eyes away from Your light.
Your infinite light brings hope to my darkness.
It is incredible to adore the look of Your face.
It is beyond words that we can step into Your gracious heart.
How madly in love I am with You.
You shine goodness and bring more goodness for me.
You bring the best out of me, pure and refined.
You satisfy me more than I can express.
Your voice calms my circumstances.
The waves of my life cannot overwhelm me.
You are always on my boat, protecting me.
You are the epicentre of all hope and comfort.
I bless you mightily where I go.
I bathe in the pools of Your anointing.
I let go completely and give all of myself to You.
I want to be like you, High One.
I love to sit next to You in the heavenlies.
Bring me to completion in You.
You are perfectly wonderful, Son of God.

Psalm 68

Earnestly will I contend for the faith.
I will not be moved to the left nor the right.
For the Lord has set me on His perfect path.
How will I move?
I am planted in His faith.
I am prepared to resist the evil doubts.
They will not shake me.
I humbly submit to my God.
He will help me.
I will not let go of what has been promised.
Time and time again He have given me victory.
Why would I fall off now? Never!
I stand firm in what He has said.
I move forward towards my promises.
My precious prizes, my goals.
He is my all in all.
The first of my life and the last of my life.
I refuse to succumb to doubt,
For if I do, I will be completely thrown off and lose my vision/
But it is my God who strengthens me to move forward
He arms me in warfare and defends me with His shield.
The enemy will have no ground,

For I set forth to conquer the trials,
Till I reach the amazing promises,
Lo, I can see the beautiful horizon.
Oh, what beauty awaits me.
There it is, my beautiful treasures.
Onward I move, with the Wind of the Spirit at my back!
I do not cease to believe Him.
I take Him at His word, and everything else is lies.
He is the supreme truth.
His Word is final!

Psalm 69

I sought the Lord for what I wanted.
He sought me for what He wanted to do instead.
I desired my promises quickly,
Yet He pruned and moulded me patiently.
I wrestled with Him day and night,
Yet He comforted and calmed my spirit.
I kept my eyes on what I desired,
Be He stood in the way of my sight.
Then I realised it was not about myself at all.
Rather, it was about His own will.
It was about His working power resting upon me.
It is good to hope for the goodness to come.
Intimacy with Him is far better.
He fulfills us whilst we wait.
He walks with us and lifts up our head.
His will is being unfolded in my life.
I take notice of all things being brought together.
I cannot ignore the movement of His hand.
He trains my patience in the wait.
I will praise and trust Him daily.
I will stive for intimacy with Him,
Rather than what He can give.

Psalm 70

I see Your footsteps next to mine,
On the sands, You walk with me.
I see You taking me into Your river,
Immersing me into Your new life.
I stand in You completed.
I remain purified and sanctified.
You lead me on paths of peace.
I am kept safe near You.
All the obstacles make way for You,
They are ruined and destroyed.
The paths are opened up through the forests.
The trees are uprooted and walk away.
The animals move and remain at peace.
Creation recognises You as You walk past.
The clouds are cleared and the sun shines upon the path.
The ground is soft and easy to tread upon.
The rocks are cast aside, there are no pits.
You teach me that when You walk with me; paths are made!
No obstacles or barriers can withstand You.
You who are able to subdue and submit,
All creation under Yourself!

Psalm 71

I have died to live,
For the sake of the living Christ.
I have emptied myself of my desires.
I long to be ruled by Christ.
I do not count myself as great.
I have become willing to do what others won't.
Following His example, I seek to raise others.
I count them greater.
I suffer for the sake of Christ.
I see that I am dust.
I release the cares of this life,
And give Him liberty to rule as Lord.
He decides the paths I take,
He leads me into His truth.
I wrestle with pride and lusts.
But my Lord commands me to crucify them.
I count myself as last.
I don't strive to be great.
He raises and lowers me as He pleases.
I die to myself daily.
The cross is heavy, but I carry it.
In a sense I am nothing,
In another; I am everything to Him.

Psalm 72

Lord, arrest my heart and my thoughts.
I do not want to curse You.
I reject any instance of doubt.
In my anger, I do not want to reject You.
I seek to remain humble and dependent on You.
My life is in Your hands.
So then how can I walk away.
Lord, change me.
Rebuke my pride and humble me.
Teach me the way of meekness and gentleness.
Prune me according to Your will.
Expand my capacity to be an example for others.
Change my heart to look like Yours.
Lead me to walk in holiness and purity.
What can I do apart from You?
I would suffer in vanity and struggle in hopelessness.
To who would I turn to? Where would I go?
I am so attached to You and Your peace.
Grace me with Your love.
Teach me to be loving towards You.
I don't want to hate You.
I don't want any barriers in our connection.
Everything else is vanity.

Psalm 73

Having an eternal perspective changes your life.
Your priorities are significantly shifted.
Everything seems unreal, and so temporary.
You begin to pay attention to how brittle and fleeting this life is.
You feel your time begin to speed up.
Your days are quicker and your sleeps are shorter.
What concerns you at present will not matter in eternity.
What you're holding onto fiercely right now, won't necessarily
follow you forever.
What is that which lasts eternal?
How short is the time to make a significant difference, to store up
treasure in heaven?
No more do you take your moments for granted.
Everywhere you go, you seek to impact and make a blessing to
others.
Wealth goes and comes, but your eternal nature will remain forever.
Would it be in a state pleasing to the Almighty?
Your deeds will follow you.
Your heart will be questioned, did you learn to love well?
Have you done what He commanded you to do daily?
Or did you waste all the time you can never get back, on such
temporary and vain things.

These lead to destruction and emptiness; it holds no weight at the
Bema of the Lamb.
Consider carefully what you shall do with what you have been
given.
Your hairs will grey sooner than you think.

Psalm 74

The Lord gives the vision.
He shares the details of the secrets of the future.
He shows you what is to come, what can be expected.
He prepares your heart ahead of time, that you may grasp the
realities of His truth.
The Lord does not lie about anything.
He will reveal where you ought to be, the end result.
He will kindle in you the fire to step forward.
He will prompt you to take the leap of faith.
Don't be afraid, He will not let you sway off the course.
The course He initiated; He will be faithful to it.
He will fill your heart with faith as you begin to take the first step.
You might go side to side, but He will lead you.
You begin to see elements falling into place.
You begin to see the details unblurring and becoming clear.
So, you can believe that He is walking with you.
He works this journey out with you, one step at a time.
You may take steps forward, and then fall backwards.
He will remain in charge and set your direction back on the path.
No one is lost in the Lord; they are always where they are meant to be.
God works things around you, and works you around things.
There is nothing surprising to Him; He asks only for your
faithfulness.
Are you prepared to walk the path and partner with His vision?
That it may come to pass in your generation.

Psalm 75

Kindle your faith.
Do not let the fire burn out.
How else will you see Him move?
You must believe.
Your faith will bring His promises to pass.
Your faith will move all obstacles.
Do not waiver in faith, contend for it earnestly.
Your faith is yours alone, it saves you.
If your faith is strong enough, others will come to be saved too.
Do you believe the truth of His word?
Does it apply to your life, according to His instructions?
Will you not believe for the sake of your soul?
Those who do not believe cannot see.
If you want to see the glory of Christ, ye must believe He is Lord.
Do not allow yourself to be stagnant, nor your heart to grow cold.
Fan the flames of it and permit it to believe for greater things.
Submit to the written Word of His truth.
Let it supercharge your faith.
You will see His signs; you will gaze upon His wonders.
He is not far; your faith will pull Him close to you.
Without your faith, not much can be accomplished.
You may fulfill great feats in your own strength, but you can do greater with faith in Him.
Where do you stand in faith?

Psalm 76

He has made it a priority;
To build His church for the purpose of retrieving the lost.
He has made it His mission,
To restore the hearts of His enemies to the kingdom of God.
He has promised to train and us and equip us,
Should we submit,
That we may share in His power and purposes, to vindicate the lost.
How great is His love for you and me,
That He would abandon His comfort and empty Himself,
So as to win you over and give you and eternal inheritance,
In a country that will never end.
His priority ought to be our priority,
May His will be our will.
That we walk in His power, to seek and save the lost.
For this purpose, Christ came and died,
We also ought to die to ourselves and agendas.
May our plans and desires be crucified.
May we be emptied of ourselves as Christ was emptied.
We follow His perfect example and bear His witness.
We operate in love and compassion, not force and brutality.
We co-labour with His Spirit; our Helper,
And focus on just one soul at a time.
The day of salvation is today, God be praised.

Psalm 77

The weaknesses of my flesh overtake me,
They run through the course of my natural actions.
I will not hide them, nor will I bury them.
I overcome shame and guilt through confession
I will boast about them all the more.
By this, the miracle nature and power of Christ may rest on my flesh;
That my weaknesses will be transformed into inspiration for others.
I will lack nothing good if He is my strength.
I will not let my weaknesses overtake me.
Though I do what I don't desire to do,
Christ will change my natural course into holiness.
The redemptive work of Christ will have its full accomplishment in me.
I am saved that I may be sanctified; continually cleansed for His appearance.
The sanctification work will not set me back, but will rid me of bad fruits.
I am content in my weaknesses as they have become my strengths.
I thank God for what I face, I am not ashamed of my trials.
He refines me as gold as they have its course.
I am perfected and lack nothing good.

One weakness at a time; I discover the loving patience of my God.
There is no condemnation, no weight in my heart, nor my shoulders.
This love and forgiveness cannot be understood,
Though I was once filthy, I am now made clean and spotless.
For this reason, He suffered and died;
That I may exchange with Him- His perfection for my filth; and I am liberated.

Psalm 78

Come back to the Father.
You don't need to be lost.
He grieves that you are in pain.
He knows your life more than anyone else, He values it.
You don't have to figure this out on your own;
You were never meant to.
He weeps when you weep,
He knows how you struggle.
He wants to restore you.
What are you pursuing in life?
Apart from Him, everything is vanity.
So why do you continue in pursuit?
There is a portion in your heart that only He can fill.
Do you not know that your life is so temporary?
Anything you attain today can be taken away tomorrow, so why do you strive so much?
Will you hold onto worldly goods forever? They will dry up and be destroyed.
The Father wants to give you eternal things.
You were made for Him.
He wants you to know Him, that you may find all things.
He wants to complete your life.
How long will you turn away?
There is nothing too filthy for Him to clean.
He wants to remove all your filth.

Psalm 79

My good God watches over me as I sleep.
He remains vigilant over me as I rest in my tent.
I am free to let go of all fear and worries.
I release myself into the care of His hand as I drift into the unconscious.
Whom do I fear? The arrow of the darkness? Surely not.
For His shield guards me in my most vulnerable state.
As I am out in the open, His angels encamp around me.
They surround me in a circle with their swords at the ready.
I depend on Him alone for my protection.
Nothing can harm me, nor come near me.
Nothing will touch me.
For I am defended by the One who is faithful.
He visits me in my dreams to fill me with hope and show me the future.
I am in a pleasant state of rest.
His Spirit recharges me.
My body is secure and so is my soul.
I thank God that He is my protector.
I thank God He has summoned His angels to guard my tent.
Evil runs away from me, their armies turn away in fear.

For the angels who guard me are fierce in battle and have fire in
their eyes.
Their swords will cut down an entire army of darkness.
Who can withstand the warrior whom God has created.
They are in service of my calling and mission.
I sleep in complete peace as the Light of the World rests upon me.

Psalm 80

The breath of God brings life.
God breathed on dust and we rose.
God breathes on the atmosphere,
It brings the radiance and weight of His presence.
Our hearts are filled with peace.
We can fall back into His arms.
God breathes on circumstances of death,
Hearts are then awakened, spirits are lifted up, the dead come to life physically and spiritually!
God breathes on a church and multitudes are added daily.
His breath brings increase!
Stagnant situations are renewed with joy and hope.
All which you see around you that lives, moves and has its operation;
That has been filled with the breath of the Lord.
Are you dead? Do you need newness of life?
Ask for God to breathe upon you for your situation.
He is the Master over all life.
Our hearts beat according to His permission.
We reflect His handiwork as we take our next breath.
He is the epicentre of all life.

Psalm 81

The real secret to living this life is focussing on Christ first.
Has He not commanded us to seek His kingdom?
He knows your desires and He will fill you in the wait.
You want something but you need to surrender it to Him first.
Surrender your desires and adopt a servant heart.
He will give you what you need and hear your future desires.
He plants desires in our heart.
Whilst you wait for something,
He will fill and make you satisfied.
When you get what you desire,
He will help you unpack it in the right way;
That you may inherit and make the most out of it.
He desires that His blessing upon you lasts a long time.
That you may have the wisdom to honour the blessing and handle it wisely.
I speak to this out of experience.
What Christ wants to do is work on your heart,
To make you ready to receive what He wants for you.
That is the secret to an abundant life.

Psalm 82

How many times is it required for a man to enter the wilderness?
As many as it takes for the refinement of the heart.
Each time there is a new lesson,
There is a new level of humility to acquire.
The Lord works tirelessly on the character and the heart of His chosen.
There are many things in a person that need to be cut out,
There are many things yet to be replaced with the things of God.
How can an impure vessel go out to minister?
How can a man who has not a firm foundation, support the foundations of others?
It is not a time to question the Lord, but to yield.
It is necessary for trials and wilderness periods.
These are there to equip and train a person.
Man goes through seasons and cycles of change,
At each stage there is more to learn and man becomes stronger.
The goal is the character development; to look like Jesus.
Though there are many costs associated;
What the Lord recompenses is far better and greater than the pain.
The man is required to get his heart right for ministry.
He is being trained to pour out into the lives of others.
Does this cup not need to be filled first?

Does this vessel not need to be polished inside and out?
The righteousness of God qualifies us to be sanctified internally.
The seeds of ministry and calling are planted in the heart of man;
the Lord waters and grows it maturely.

Psalm 83

Moment by moment, the Word of God stands.
He is true in all our circumstances.
You must trust Him!
Do not despise the trials,
Do not lose your hope in the quiet.
He is true to you amid chaos.
Rest assured; He will still have His way.
He is the only One who is consistent.
He will hold you in His hand and bear you up.
He guards your feet that you may not stumble.
Trust in Him, for the sake of your welfare.
Keep leaning on Him.
He is waiting in the background for your benefit.
You will see His glory if you keep persisting.
Yes, I know it is difficult at times.
Trials bring growth in us and perfection.
Spiritual resilience is an exercise.
Allow Him to train you up, that you may not depart from His path.
He is preparing you for what is to come.
It is not up to you to bring His promises to pass.
It is His, and His only to do so.
You remain faithful to Him.

Psalm 84

For each day, I walk in the blessings of Christ, and my spirit is full.
I have wholesome encounters and many encouragements.
My joy is full, and I remain at peace.
When I retire for the night and awake next morning,
I am 'empty'.
Many a morning have I awoken and felt the need to nourish my spirit again.
I do not know where this emptiness comes from.
Am I robbed in the night?
I sought the Lord for clarity into this.
He showed me that there is a need for the daily bread.
There is a sense of 'reset' at each day.
I hunger and thirst for Him and His filling all over again at each dawn.
I do not understand this mystery.
What takes it away during my sleep?
Or is this another method the Lord uses to keep me dependant on Him.
I have learnt that a life committed to Christ, must be fully dependant on Him.
IN ALL THINGS.
Even the smallest things require the counsel of the Lord.

He needs to be involved in my plans, the decisions I make; that I may fulfill them according to His will.
Beginning my day without Him can throw off my whole morning.
It can be burdensome, yet it is an opportunity to practise the good faith.
I know He waits for me at first light.

Psalm 85

He tenderises my heart and softens it,
Before He fills me with more of Him.
The tender heart is able to be more receptive to Him.
He softens me internally to fill me with more of His love.
That I may abound in grace, love and power for the next level.
What can He do with a heart that's closed?
The Lord prepares me to be elevated.
I am faced with internal grief but I handle it better than the last.
See how He progress and builds me.
He only gives me what I can handle;
By this I am comforted.
I am being stretched, and my capacity is expanding.
He has answered the prayer of Jabez.
He continues to do new things.
I cannot anticipate His next step.
He is measuring my faith.
He tests the motives of my heart.
His hand is heavily upon me; I cannot escape it.
I continuously give Him the growing pains.
He makes righteousness to bloom in me.

Psalm 86

Each one of us is called to bear our own cross,
We stand in a line together as the armies of the King.
In this world, justified, yet struggling with the flesh and trials.
To each person's life, is allotted their own troubles.
This is what Christ has informed,
Thru trials and sorrows, we will not fear for He has overcome the world?
Therefore, are we called to overcome or sink deeper into destruction?
We are afflicted but we remain steadfast.
This is the life, for our discipline and virtues' sake, we humble ourselves under pressure,
That He may give us the grace to carry our cross.
The first One who carried the cross made it till the very end.
He kept His joy before Him, with His eyes upon the promise of God.
Therefore, in like manner, we keep our eyes upon our example,
And remind ourselves daily of His precious promises;
Why we do what we do.
Why we are who we are.
Because the Son commands it; and we are made worthy of our calling.
We are made worthy of the kingdom.

Through pains, burdens, challenges, pressures, hardships, suffering, and then overcoming:
We are called to enter His kingdom.
We can count on His promises, no matter how heavy the cross on our back.
He did it, so we can do it too.

Psalm 87

No more grief, but joy.
No more sorrow, but dancing.
No more regret, but hope.
No more pain, but relief.
No more hopelessness but hope for the future.
No more isolation but belonging.
No more rejection, but acceptance.
No more separation, but oneness.
No more darkness, but absolute light.
No more shadows, when the light is above all.
No more anxiety, but perfect peace.
No more poverty but possessing everything.
No more lack, but abundance in all areas.
No more vanity, but full meaning.
No more unnecessary suffering, but testimonies upon testimonies.
No more insecurity, but boldness and confidence.
No more broken hearts but filled with strength to overcome.
No more temporary fixes, but eternal solutions.
No more shame, but full reconciliation.
No more lightness but having wings to soar like eagles.
Set apart and raised up to be the lights of the world;
How great is our inheritance; co heirs with Jesus.
No more eternal darkness but forever a home in His eternal
    kingdom;
Bright forever.

Psalm 88

Give to the Lord freely,
Do not withhold anything from Him.
Search yourself, what can you give to Him for worship?
Look to others, what can you give to others for His glory?
As we give and make sacrifices, He is honoured amongst us.
Look at what He has given for you,
To liberate you and make you His own.
Has He not given up that which was most precious to Him?
Do not rob the Lord, nor withhold from Him what is due.
Humble yourself therefore, and recognise that all you have comes from Him.
Your skills, your knowledge, your intellect and capacity to generate wealth.
Does it come from your lineage, or does it come from yourself?
Has He not fashioned you in His image?
All good things come from above, the Father of lights supplies all.
He sharpens us and quickens us; that we may be effective in our giftings.
What we are good at, we ought to do it for His service.
Nothing temporary is for us to gain completely,
We have already gained everything through Jesus.

Renew your mind and discover what is most important in eternal value.
What you have; thank God for it and be faithful in it,
That He may trust you to carry a greater capacity.
Then use what you have in His leading to build the kingdom;
For through offerings; obedience and following our calling; we build His kingdom.

Psalm 89

The prophet declares 'The Lord has come',
He prepares the way for the entry of the King.
The earth shakes and strongholds crumble.
The skies are split open.
Eyes are pierced with the blinding flames of His majesty.
The Light of Life shines His rays across the lands, canvassing it in purity.
The foundations of the earth cry out and shake as it sees its Creator.
The apostles come together to receive their Reward.
They show the Lord the communities they have prepared for Him.
They show the paths they have paved for others to journey upon.
They say 'All our roads lead to You, O Lord who holds all life in Your hands'
Others follow them also.
They have come to bring with them the people they served, the ones they loved.
The prophet echoes the heart of God for the nations, 'Holy and purity I observe. Realize Who I am.'
The inhabitants are spread out from left to the right.
The righteous ones run toward Him and the wicked cower in their shame.

The Lord observes that the pillars of His ministry have laboured to
add.
The persecuted accompany the train of His robe.
His fold has grown and multiplied.
The eyes of the Lord remain upon His people; His heart loves them
eternally.
I see the Lord shepherding His sheep into the gold gates of heaven.
O' what a sight to behold; I am filled in awe.

Psalm 90

The kingdom of heaven is inside of you;
What a mystery, but clear with the enlightened eyes.
When you have the revelation of Christ in your heart;
You will realise that the kingdom He created dwells within you.
This is to speak of the culture and the essence of His kingdom.
Until it is time for the coming kingdom of God to manifest in the world,
It dwells within the heart of every believer.
Christ has taken the throne of the hearts of His people.
From which He rules and directs the believer's life in the ways of the kingdom.
To the one who lives according to the will of God; the kingdom is displayed in his conduct and faith.
To the one who has lost his life for the gain of Christ;
Christ manifests Himself in him and the revelation of the kingdom comes alive.
The hearts are enlightened and understanding is given.
It is like living in two worlds at once.
To be alive in the spirit is to be in touch with heaven.
The more sensitive one is to the Spirit, the more they see heaven.
The Father seeks to reveal the kingdom to mankind.
The heart is the doorway to seeing the kingdom.

The throne of the heart must be given over the Lord,
That it may be unlocked to see God in His glory.
The kingdom is alive and will never end.
It will continue to sweep across the lands.
The kingdom is accessible, not far.
Did not Christ say not to look here or there?
It cannot be seen with the naked eye,
But only can be captured with the surrendered heart.
All that Christ is; is the kingdom of God made manifest.
The culture of the kingdom is of purity, holiness and service.
When man enacts in these; he lives out the kingdom and it is manifested in his life.
This is done that others may believe there is a higher world than ours.
The world is modelled after the kingdom; this is a lesser country.
Heaven will take over earth one day.
The righteous ones prepare their hearts for this,
And live their lives according to the pleasure of God.
They know they have an eternal place with God.
They feel the warmth of kingdom living in their hearts.
They cannot turn back to the fallen state of the world.
For they have been identified with Christ,
And are called to rule and reign with the Son of God.
He makes us to be priests, and then kings unto His God.
The kingdom of heaven grows from a mustard seed.

It is watered in the hearts of all those who believe.
They go to the corners of the world to spread His kingdom.
It then grows and bears kingdom fruit.
So much so that the world will never be able to contain it.
How can it?
It is everlasting and everlasting.

Psalm 91

The one who depends on God,
Will make his dwelling under His protective covering.
The Lord is the one I rely on for everything.
He will keep me safe from all traps.
He will secure me from all sickness.
His hand remains on me and safeguards my coming and going.
He is my only shield; who defends all my blind spots.
No evil shall visit me at night,
Nor will any attack be successful towards my life.
All will crumble around me but I will remain steadfast in Him.
I will witness what the wicked reap.
I have made my God my sanctuary,
Therefore, all evil cowers and flees my sight.
I sense His angels encircling me.
They are present in my times of warfare and they guide me to
triumph.
They walk with me and protect me in unseen ways.
I have authority to trample evil as all things are under His feet.
He will always work to deliver me, protect me and preserve my life.
I will live long in the land as His saved one;
I will always remain in Him until He calls me home.

Psalm 92

Sometimes He is so quiet,
I can barely hear Him.
His voice can be so soft,
You'd need to run into a cave to hear it.
Sometimes He is so loud I can't run away from it.
I hear it everything so clearly as speaking to another man.
His still small voice makes me to silence all distraction;
That I may hear Him and learn to know His voice.
Sometimes He speaks little enough for me to train my faith;
That I may grow to trust Him and seek His voice in everything.
"I am never completely silent, but speak also in other ways", says the Lord.
He draws me closer when He draws back purposefully.
He can be trusted in the darkness as in the light.
Oh, how He has been faithful to me despite missing the marks.
He will make Himself known in the noise.
Some days, He only speaks when I acknowledge Him.
Even then He reminds me to look for Him.
Some days He speaks as soon as my eyes are open from sleep.
Listen not only with your ears but with your heart.
Hear what He is saying to you this season.
He never sleeps.
He always speaks.
He can be trusted.

Psalm 93

"I will be good towards you,
I will be gracious towards you.
When you fall down, I will keep you.
I will raise you up stronger than ever.
I will not forsake my own.
I will tend to you, my child.
I know you by name and I know everything in you.
When you sleep, I see you and guard you.
I will not cause you to lack but have sufficiency in the things you need.
I know your heart; I see within you and I can read between the lines.
I know your every intent.
I look to bless you and encourage you in all things good.
I know the way you take and I will gently redirect you if you step off the path.
The path I have for you is unique, no one else can tread upon it.
I built you in a special way; I formed you with loving and tender care.
I see your struggles and I use them to make goodness abound toward you.
Have no doubt, I will help your faith and cause you to overcome.
I have built you to be triumphant.
I call you into deeper intimacy.

I pursue you continually and I long to love you tangibly.
Would you stop for a moment and look to me?
I seek to envelope you in my perfect love, that you may know what it truly feels to be accepted.
Despite your past I accept you.
I call you home.
It is not enough for Me that you would have a head knowledge of Me.
I deeply desire that you would come home fully.
Abide in Me.
Taste and see that I am good towards you.
Make Me your dwelling place that you may walk in the fullness of life.
I want you to know what it truly means to live.
I have shaped you for a specific destiny.
I am moulding you daily and fashioning you after my intent.
If you are not already mine; then I want you to realise I died to win you over.
I want you just as you are.
You don't have to offer me anything spectacular; just give me your heart.
I will make you flourish in all your ways.
You will experience true wholeness and completion.
I desire that you would remain close to me continually.
Pursue and seek My face daily.
Know Me intimately.

I have already created the bright path forward.
There is no barrier to knowing me and coming toward me.
I am open and ready to be received by you.
Allow me to make my home in your heart.
I seek to save you; I seek to love you infinitely.
I seek to show you the purpose for which you are alive.
I seek to be one with you",
Says the Lord to His creation.

Psalm 93

Wake up prophets!
Arise from your slumber!
Prophets in training awake!
Mature prophets awake!
Hearken your ears to the voice of the Lord,
Listen to what He is saying.
Receive the Word of the Lord in season.
Let the company of prophets be assembled.
Let revival come through the mouth of the prophets.
Prophets of all ages and nations; this is your time.
Do not shy away from your call.
The Lord has made you a prophet to the nations.
Release the freedom of God through His word over the nations.
Do not fear man.
Take hold of your calling; being trained in righteousness.
Present your ears as offerings to the Lord; and your mouth to be weapons.
You are being sharpened; you are being refined.
Your words reveal the Father's heart and bring correction to those who are falling.
Speak boldly because you have an office of authority.
You are a pillar of the church; a gift to the body.

Without prophets we have no vision; the church cannot move forward.
Know your role and submit to His mighty hand.
Do not doubt, but persevere.
Your life is being preserved.
You no longer belong to yourself.
Live for the living God; you are separated for a while.
In the wilderness you learn to discern His voice.
He will break you forward unto greater things.
He will fly you to the nations if required.
Speak and usher in His presence.
Look at the Baptist!
So make way for His feet in the same manner.
Lay down the gold carpet for the Lord Jesus.
Bow and submit.
Welcome Him into the regions He has given to you.
He is Lord.
You are His prophet.
Take up your mantle and arise.
Be His living stone.

Psalm 94

Each of us who are in the Beloved can hear Him.
We are given the capacity to recognise His voice.
The scripture emphasizes we are His sheep.
We follow the leading of the Great Shepherd.
When we are distracted by the false lights of the world,
We can go astray and lose track of His voice.
Yet, He remains faithful.
He keeps His eyes on us even when we fall into pits and traps.
He sees us and continues to speak to us.
Whether we hear it or not, He speaks.
Jesus in faithful to us in all regards.
We have antennas in our hearts.
In our free will, we choose to receive heaven's broadcasts,
Or to be distracted with temporary concerns.
The person who has the Lord in his heart or ear shall never go off track.
This can be a difficult discipline,
But He is gracious and covers us in love.
He knows the path we take.
Our hearts and ears shall come forth as gold.

Psalm 95

By His stripes I am healed.
He has already paid for my healing and restoration; there is no barrier.
I continue to walk in ever-increasing health.
My body prospers through Christ in my inner man.
My body is aligned to the will of God.
My mind is renewed upon His truth.
My soul is merged to His spirit.
I am fully rejuvenated.
My heart is resurrected.
The power of Christ flows in my mortal body.
All attacks from the enemy do not reach me.
They are carried away like leaves in the wind.
Though the frequency of the attacks of the opposition increases;
I remember 'greater is He in me'.
Christ and I are the majority.
His Word says I have victory in all areas.
I will lift up the Lord before my attackers.
They will flee in despair.
The light in me will penetrate their darkness.
I have every advantage over the enemy.
The shield of faith permits me to hold fast.
I stay grounded on His Word.
I see my feet developing roots and going into His written word.
I exalt Him.

Psalm 96

Despite setbacks or isolation,
My hope will rest in the Lord.
I actively pursue Him in my trials and pains.
Physical pain cannot overcome me.
I am one with Him forever;
As He is, so am I.
I conquer along with Him.
He goes before me to set my path straight.
He covers my blind spots.
I am His representative in all nations and places.
My authority increases in each area of victory.
My capacity is enlarged.
I am anxious for nothing; I cast my concerns upon Him.
He makes me stronger than I am.
No arrow or trap can stop me in my tracks.
We are approached by battles but we break through.
How do we move forward in pain?
We keep our eyes on Him and pain flees.
We speak life and pain has no place.
We know our identity and stand firm in it.
We will not be thrown in the wind but will remain rooted and firm in Him.
He is our eternal hope.

Psalm 97

He has appointed me as a leader to thousands.
He has given me a rod of authority to lead the masses.
Multitudes will hearken to my voice,
As I proclaim His gospel to the nations.
They will hear my authority as I bring freedom to them.
I am anointed to bring the Lord's deliverance.
All chains are off in Jesus' name.
I am fully empowered in every regard.
Look, He has sent me to run crusades.
He has sent me to demonstrate His power before the unbelievers.
He has set me on a high rock and awarded my life with great things.
He has made my name as one to remember.
He is preparing me to leave an everlasting legacy.
I will lead other leaders as I step out in authority.
I will reflect His victory to the downcast.
I will show them His glory.
I will embark upon journeys to the far ends of the earth.
I will bring many of them home with me.

Psalm 98

The Lord orders the seasons of life.
He decrees the timeframes with their own purposes.
A life given to Him is one not in man's control.
For the Lord is given liberty to build up or remove for His purposes.
He is in charge during the storms and He remains watchful over the
life of His Beloved.
Though He seems to be far,
He tests the heart of a person.
Who is truly faithful to Him?
Who calls Him Lord and is truly willing to surrender all?
All seasons have their own purposes in a person's life.
Faith, patience and declarations will carry a man to breakthrough.
The waves continue to rise against but you must remain steadfast.
He commands you to be strong and have great courage.
He is at your right hand.
Endure and continue to stand.
He declares His faithfulness over you and counts you resilient.
He will carry you and reward you every time.

Psalm 99

It is the true pursuit of the Lord that matters.
One must learn to differentiate what He can give,
And who He is.
They are not the same.
We ought to know Him more.
Deeper relationship and communion with Him is what He desires.
It is what He died for.
It is good to expect His promises but we cannot make our desires an idol.
We must continually examine our hearts.
We ought to remain in His love and keep Him first above all.
He must be the main driving force of our lives.
He must be the source of all we do and how we live.
We are chasing the wind if we seek anything apart from Him.
What then shall be our end?
Are we not called to grow in union with and know Him deeper?
Surrender is a process and we must be diligent in giving Him glory.
The less of you which exists,
Gives Him more room to show His face in your face.

Psalm 100

I wake up with my eyes set upon the Lord,
Convicted of His nature of grace and glory.
Knowing full well the one thing which satisfies my soul,
His eternal presence following me wherever I go.
I am made complete in Him and only when I recognise Him.
I have come to know that everything out of His presence is worth nothing.
Everything away from Him is so empty.
He has convicted my heart to know the truth of His word;
That I may rise in the knowledge of Him and intimacy thereof.
I am set in the ways of the Lord.
He has taught me to consider my life as nothing so precious to myself.
I seek to complete the course He has set before me.
The race must be complete,
Along with the ministry I have received from Christ.
I am fully convicted that He and His work matter so much,
That I may lose all I have to gain Him as my eternal reward.
Oh, how my soul thirsts after Him and it continues to yearn,
Because He is eternal and never-ending.
There is so much to learn and so much to gain in Him.
There is so much to grow in Him.

He is like a well which never runs dry and His water is more and more nourishing each time.
I must finish the course of my life; and have set my eyes upon the stars.
I will fly; so Spirit, carry me.

Psalm 101

I have softened my heart towards my God,
That I may receive more from Him;
That I may be intimate with Him.
He has taken me through a great refinement.
I have sought the Lord continually,
Thru my pains and victories.
He has not shifted nor changed towards me.
I am brought closer to Him daily.
My soul aches if I am not with Him.
My mind and thoughts keep chasing the Lord.
He has restricted my path to Him alone.
I cannot move off the path,
For there is nothing else that could fill me.
I have realised the goodness of God in pain;
That He is my faithful other half.
I have realised Jesus in me,
Who is my strength and confidence.
I cannot be apart from Him.
I hold fast to His promises.
He waits for me in the morning and rushes in when I seek Him.
Who is like the Lord who continually satisfies me?
I cannot live without Him.

Psalm 102

Lord, I seek You.
I thirst for You.
My hunger grows strongly.
I desire more glory encounters.
Flood my life with Your presence.
When You manifest, it is the best feeling ever.
I am filled with awe and excitement.
Only You can satisfy me.
Come Lord Jesus and manifest.
Make Yourself known and appear,
That I may behold Your glory,
And my face shall shine like the sun.
You are the brightest star I have ever seen.
You are the most beautiful I have ever known.
You are my first love.
You hold me together and make me complete.
No human is good enough to complete me.
Only You can never fail.
I seek to know You, Lord.
I want to be strengthened by You.
Call me forward.
Mature me as Your son.
I seek to love and serve You.
You are the most excellent to me.

Psalm 103

You are the most excellent of all Lord.
You are the eternal and true God.
Lord, You are excellent and worthy of worship.
You are supreme and mighty to save.
I have not seen You.
But my heart has known You forever.
Who can remain standing when the glory of God is revealed?
All observe His splendour and remain in awe.
Our great God reigns true and supreme.
My best friend and my constant companion,
Jesus my brother.
I long to know You more.
I want to see the power of Your Hand.
You heal and restore without fail.
I honour You deeply and my heart is for You.
How incredible You are.
You are the God of eternity.
All flesh bows to You.
All spirits and materials confess Your Lordship.
You spoke and all creation came to be.
Who can contend with my best friend?
My beautiful advocate, precious High Priest.

Psalm 104

Precious Lamb, You are faithful.
You are trustworthy.
You complete what You start.
You keep me on the path.
When I veer off, You bring me back.
When I stumble, You help me up.
You reposition me as You see fit.
You establish my path and journey.
How amazing it is that You go before me?
My life belongs to You.
I boast all the more in You and Your glory.
You never let go of my Hand.
You are true to everything You say.
Though there may be troubles, You deliver me.
You stop those who try to stop me.
You are careful over my life;
You are cautious to what enters it.
You protect me at the roots of my foundation.
You seek to see me grow;
So You set me on a great journey which will shape me.
You are my Potter and the Author of my life.

Psalm 105

Jesus is my destiny.
I have sought countless times to look for the Way,
Whilst I have been lost in the dark.
I have stumbled countless times and looked for the true Light.
My Bright and Morning Star,
How dear You are to me.
You encompass all that I need.
You are the construct and fine blueprint of my life.
You weave everything carefully for me.
You are the dearest of my heart.
I hope in You continually and daily I mediate upon Your Words.
I remember all the names given to You and recognise Your authority over all.
I find my way upon the true path again and again.
Precious Holy Spirit takes my hand and leads me back.
There is no condemnation for my stumbling.
He does not scold me but lovingly corrects me.
He lifts me upon His shoulders and carries me upon the waves of life.
The waters are roaring and the winds are strong,
But Jesus walks on it and holds me carefully.

With strength He commands eternal 'peace', and everything
subsides.
My path is then revealed again and I can see it straight and narrow.
I follow the Bright and Morning star into my eternal destiny.
Jesus is my brother.

Psalm 106

I trust in you O God of my salvation.
Even though man my fail me, You are my compass,
Forever pointing me to a certain hope
You are the anchor of my life,
The lifeboat of my being.
You are forever at my right side, reminding me of my destiny.
See to it Lord, that I continue to press on.
I cannot carry myself, therefore I need Your Hands.
Carry me and show me the truthful part, cut out between the rocks.
Show me the true way, the straight and narrow one.
Be the handles at side and do no permit me to fall off course.
Keep the blinders on my sides, lest I look away.
Forever walk before me and keep Yourself in my sights.
Step by step, you lead me.
You beckon me along the treacherous paths.
You give my soul rest along the quiet paths.
I see Your Shepherd's rod and staff at work.
You use them to train me.
Though I fall, I fall forward and never to the side.
You raise me up quickly and I become stronger.
"Onward to destiny", saith the Lord.
"How wondrous and mighty art the plans I have for thee;
If thou could see it, thou would run along the beaches shouting
praises and raising hands in joy forever"

Psalm 107

The wheels of the chariot spin,
And they keep spinning as the warrior of truth rides into battle.
He is adorned with the armour of the living God,
And his countenance is like the Son.
Bright and filled with living light.
He is the one who is steadfast in the tides of battle, waging war against the standard of evil.
He is immovable when the Heavenly King rides at his right side.
He has no fear but is fully focussed on the victory which has been won.
He keeps his sights on the sword of the Lord.
He is given the bow of the angels, and the arrows of the kings of heaven.
The Lord is his watchful Shield which guards his back.
The wheels of the chariot continue to spin as he rides forth to do battle.
O, who can withstand the path way of the anointed warrior.
The one who has put on the Lord Jesus Christ.
He wears the fullness of Christ's deity; who has all rule and power.
His enemies flee at his coming as they see the heavenly angels riding behind the warrior.

The tides of the battle shift and change rapidly as the wheels of the chariot cover more and more ground.
All are subjected to the fire of the living God, and the impure are burnt till there is nothing.
No evil shall stand in the sight of the anointed warriors.
We who live in the footsteps of Jesus carry his sword to the ends of the earth.
Victory is His and the chariot wheels spin forever forward.

Psalm 108

Pour out your fire O God.
Pour out your living fire.
Burn up the world of all filth and evil.
Purify us with your living fire.
You, who are supreme.
You stand tall and reign forever.
You carry your fire in your countenance.
It is interwoven into your being.
Your shape, though like a man, is adorned with bright flames.
Flames that cannot be contained.
At your will O God, you consume.
Nothing can stand against it.
Only those who are sanctified, you do not burn.
You cannot burn your own flesh, nor your own hearts.
These you save because they have become joined to You.
You will not lose those who live in Your hands.
They are the ones You also fill with fire to burn up the nations with
Your glory.
They are your flame carriers and they light up everyone they love.
Send forth your living flames.
Show the world Your love but also display Your power.
The fiery Hand of God grasps the world anytime He wants.
He arrests every heart which is ignorant.
Nothing can stop the coming of the Son of fire.

Psalm 109

Nothing is enough for the one who lives out of the realm of this world.
There is nothing this world can give that can fill his soul.
No pleasure, no vice, no commodity, no fortune, no spouse, no friendship.
Once he has been separated from the world he must learn to live in the care of God.
His nourishment comes from the Lord, who made the man's shape.
This one has come to the end of himself, and the end of his worldly pleasure.
Anything is this world is only a temporary and false thing.
He is so hungry for what only God can give him.
Replenish his storage with your bread Lord.
The hunger pangs grow all the more.
He has no choice but to maintain his course in the Lord's path.
Nothing else can satisfy.
Help him Lord he thirsts after you.
Look at how he cries to you day and night for You to fill him.
Be merciful and complete him Lord.
His only shelter is You.
His way of life is You.
He has made everything he knows, thinks and feels, all about You.

And You call him blessed, for You promise that he shall be filled.
What a beautiful way to live;
In the realms of heaven.
Truly this world is empty and forever fading.
Only He can fill.

Psalm 110

Even if the Lord does not speak, I will maintain my course.
Even when I do not sense His presence, I will continue the course.
I stand on the basis that He is faithful,
For His word is truth and He cannot deny Himself.
He will not leave me, no matter what I feel.
My feelings are deceptive; they are not based on truth.
Only truth is the Word, that which I seek daily.
He leads me into all truth, knowledge and understanding for His purposes.
That I may grow into the likeness of His nature and character.
He promises me good even when I do not see Him.
I urge myself to continue down this path.
He hides while I seek Him.
A beautiful game which propels me forward.
He trains me to seek, which means the world to Him.
Yet, He is closer to me than a brother.
His very essence cannot depart from me.
Some trials last days, other weeks, perhaps more.
I only know to do the same thing regardless of what I feel.
The discipline and maturity aspects of my character grow.
They are pleasing to His sight.
I seek to please Him continually despite trials and tribulations.
Loneliness is a lie which I do not adopt.
My feelings lie to me, but His truth doesn't.
I am with Him, and He with me always.

Psalm 111

To the one true God I give my worship.
To the one true God I give my praise.
To the one true God, I bow down.
Lord, I lay all things at your feet.
You are the holiest one, O Lord.
I seek You only.
You are the food to my soul.
I live for your bread.
I revere You.
I long to see Your glory.
You are so powerful, Lord Jesus.
You have such great strength.
Wisdom and power are yours forever.
O Lord, you are my hope.
My shelter and my covering.
I long that all the world sees Your glory.
How bright is your countenance.
You are the world's light.
Our ray of hope.
Eternal prince and bright morning star.
Hail Lord Jesus.

Psalm 112

Dear child,
You are not lost.
You don't have to be alone.
The Shepherd is calling you home.
He bids you to come.
Run back into His arms.
It is His will that you are saved.
He longs for your embrace.
He pursues you without fail.
You can see Him at each corner.
He gave His all for you.
He would do it again for you.
The work is finished.
Everything eternal can be yours.
Would you lay down your pride?
Come and see His goodness.
Come and taste His love.
He wants to see you prosper.
You will soon realise this world is empty.
Let Him cover you and love you.
He has chosen you.
Would you choose His love over everything else?

Only He is eternal.
Everything you have will soon fade.
Don't miss out on eternal life.
You can be His and He can be yours.
Let Him lead you beside the still waters.
Go into His pasture.
Meet Him while He waits for you.

Psalm 113

There's no limit to what He can do.
There's nothing He cannot think of.
He sees all possibilities.
There are no limits with His pathways.
He is the master orchestrator.
He makes all things to take place simultaneously.
He coordinates all changes in the natural and unseens.
Man cannot put God in a box.
He operates the galaxies and the worlds at the same time.
Who can think or work like the Lord?
He operates in all realities.
He is victorious in every alternative.
He defeats death in all timelines.
He exists in more places than one.
He defeats death in all timelines.
He exists in more places than one.
He exists beyond the confines of time.
He creates new realms for His pleasure.
Yet in all these things, He is interested in us.
He loves to commune with the lowly.
He has many secrets to share.
He wants to take us out into the universe.

He wants to remove our thinking in our limitations.
And give us eyes to see into eternity.
As we are in Him, we will never stop exploring.
We have eternity to engage with Him in seeing all His creation.
We will travel with Him beyond time and space.
Behold the King over all the worlds, universes and timelines.
The endless God.

Psalm 114

He calms the waters,
The storms raging in your mind,
He calls them to be still.
He is good and kind.
He gives you peace.
No matter how high the waves climb,
He calms your waters.
So that you can see and behold Him.
He promises peace, not as the world giveth.
He guards your boat,
As you cross the oceans of life.
He holds you close to Himself,
With His hand over your raft.
He provides passage and calls the winds to be still.
He sees your coming and going,
And determines to keep you safe.
There is no wave that can overtake you.
Nothing can sink your boat.
He walks on the water close to you.
You can see Him very close.
He has conquered the seas,
And so will you.

The kingdoms of the depths are submitted,
When they see the soles of His pierced feet,
Walking upon the waves.
They retreat down to the depths,
Shaken with the fear of the Lord.
And truly so,
For all evil fears His sight and they depart quickly.
They retreat forever.
They vow never to disturb the boats of His servants,
Who make peaceful voyage,
In the company of the Creator.

Psalm 115

He has a plan.
Let the words of His promises comfort you.
He has a vision for you.
He seeks that you prosper.
He desires for you to know Him more.
His love resets your life daily.
You are always afforded a fresh start,
Because His mercies are new every morning.
He wants you to discover His plan.
He wants you to seek Him diligently.
He has rewards for you.
The kingdom of heaven is open to you.
Its gates are white open.
The clouds have made a pathway before you.
A series of steps.
His angels will guide you there.
he has prepared every encounter,
every vision and every open door.
He beckons you forward into His plan.
He desires your heart.
He has chosen you to step on a high rock.
He has called you to utter His name,

To speak His word to the nations.
Step forth into the fullness of Him who has known you.
Before time even began,
He gave you the victory.
He knew you by name.
You will always win,
But only in Him.

Psalm 116

He has a plan.
Let the words of His promises comfort you.
He has a vision for you.
He seeks your prosperity.
He desires that you would know Him more.
His love resets your life daily.
You are always afforded a fresh start each morning.
He wants you to discover His plan.
He wants you to seek Him diligently.
He has rewards for you.
The kingdom of heaven is open to you.
The path is laid before you.
He has prepared every encounter,
Every vision and every open door.
He beckons you forward into His plan.
He desires your heart.
He has chosen you to step on a high rock.
He has called you to utter His name,
To speak His word to the nations.
Step forth into the fullness of Him who has known you.
Before time even began,
He gave you the victory and the confidence to walk in Him.
You will always win,
But only in Him.

Psalm 117

The eyes of the Lord cover the world.
He sees all His own.
The Lord wants to say-
He sees you.
In your joy, He sees you.
In your pain, He sees you.
In your bed, He sees you.
In your work, He sees you.
In your tears, He sees you.
In your loneliness, He sees you.
In your asking, He sees you.
In your worship, He sees you.
In your surrender, He sees you.
In your sickness, He sees you.
In your prayer, He sees you.
In your secret place, He sees you.
In your travels, He sees you.
In your testing, He sees you.
In your sacrifice, He sees you.
In your obedience, He sees you.
In your serving, He sees you.
In your giving, He sees you.

In your family, He sees you.
Amongst your friends, He sees you.
With your relationships, He sees you.
In your singleness, He sees you.
The Word of God says,
"The eyes of the Lord are upon the righteous."
He is always seeing how to help you,
How to grow you,
And how to love you.

Psalm 118

The music of heaven pours out into the earth.
The sound waves of glory cover the atmosphere.
Heaven dances to every angelic song.
The worship bands of heaven play all day long.
The church on earth worships Him also.
They join heaven in continuous praise.
They lock hearts in the spirit, praising God.
New songs are created in holy collaboration.
God is glorified in every realm.
Every creature worships Him also.
The various realms are covered in glory.
They are filled with melodies of passion and awe.
They hear the heartfelt praises of His people.
His created beings cry out in adoration.
O how holy is the Creator God.
O how worthy is His son.
Every knee is bowed down before Him.
Every instrument is played with diligence,
To make a perfect sound of worship,
As is due to the perfection of God.
No eye has seen such excellent beauty,
That causes each man to gaze in awe.

Each being is frozen in state,
As they behold the beauty of His wings.
They see the passion of love in His eyes.
They feel the radiance of His love.
He is covered in brightness and adorned in gold.
As man worships, the golden flakes of glory are released.
His presence is poured out everywhere into all realms,
As a river that can never end.

Psalm 119

The earth sings worthy.
The earth sings glory.
Cry out to Him all you people.
Make your voices known in His courts.
He wants to hear your personal songs.
He wants to cover His throne with your worship.
It is an incense that floods His house above.
He wants to see His people sing.
His Spirit will stir His bride to worship.
Worship Him in spirit and truth.
Make heaven respond to earth.
Engage with Him, O you people.
This is a call to worship.
Be anointed with His oil and learn to praise Him.
Form your bands, prepare your strings.
Come together as one accord.
Play your sounds and sing in the spirit.
Give Him your truest form.
Call to Him in prayer and make His name great.
His is so worthy of all worship.
Seek Him continually and make His name known.
To each of you He has attributed talents.

Use them to worship in spirit and truth.
Give Him your giftings and let Him stir you.
Set your heart on fire to burn before Him.
Give Him your purest dance.
Rise up on eagles' wings and fly to Him.
Ride the waves of His melody,
Into the loving arms of God.
Forever He is worthy!

Psalm 120

The fires of heaven rain down upon the earth.
They burn endlessly consuming all unholiness.
He is coming with burning fire,
To cleanse the world from all filth.
He is cleansing and purifying all man.
The fires cannot be contained.
He is setting His holy ones alight.
They will carry His flame to all the earth.
They will radiate His heat from their hands.
They will command the obedience to faith.
They will rid the lands of evil and darkness.
They will bind the serpents with holy fire.
The wheels of His chariot are soaked in His flames.
He will ride over the world and clear out unholiness.
The earth is His to cleanse.
Man, and creatures are His to cleanse.
His fire never ends,
His eyes are filled with blue fire.
He looks upon a thing, and it sets alight.
No one is hidden from His sight.
And He is coming again to purify.
To burn up all evil forever.
Holy fire, come!
Lord Jesus, come!

Psalm 121

Even if we suffer,
We bounce back.
Even if for a short time,
We will find our reprieve in Him.
We get to rest and have resets with Him.
Even if we are exhausted,
He is never far away.
He always holds us and brings us through.
He has said that He will never leave us.
So, what concern do we have?
Let Him carry us through.
It is not always our battle to fight.
It is for Him to contend.
But it is for us to endure.
We must trust!
Moses sought Him who was invisible.
Let us do the same.
We are soldiers of Christ called to endure,
For the glory of His name.
He will see us through,
Because He is faithful and true.
He keeps His word to us.

He renews our strength.
We become stronger each time.
Our muscles grow with each suffering.
He makes us strong to lead.
So, we can show others how to conquer.
It is very liberating to overcome.
We are world overcomers as He is.
Let us suffer well for His glory.
Heaven's rewards are greater than our costs.

Psalm 122

Come to the fount and drink.
Come to the river and be refreshed.
Come to be washed by Him.
Come and seek His face.
Go the source of all things.
Keep your soul quenched with His strength.
For He sustains our spirits.
He preserves our lives.
Know the Lord and know Him well.
Come and experience His goodness.
He is passionate towards us who seek Him.
As we seek His face, we see things clearly.
He removes the blinders from our eyes,
So that we can see the truth of all things.
No deception can overtake us.
No other source can distract us.
We are rooted and grounded in Him.
We endure as seeing the One who is invisible.
In what other way can we endure?
The river flows endlessly.
There is more than enough for humanity.
Al, who are thirsty, let them come.

He has promised that they shall be filled.
They will not lack anything, nor miss out;
On what the Lord wants them to see.
The true Creator God in all His strength,
Shall be the quencher of all souls.
Those who seek shall always find.
They shall have their rewards.
The river will always flow,
From the throne of the Creator.

Psalm 123

I have sought the Lord and found favour in His sight.
I have been diligent to pursue Him with all might.
I have remembered His goodness day and night.
I have studied His Word continuously,
To the point that the Word begins to read to me.
I have called His name relentlessly.
He has raised me up to His inner circle and brought me close,
Where we can meet face to face.
He can see me clearly,
And I His precious face.
I cannot escape His sight and am held accountable.
Be there's so much grace and favour in His eyes.
He proves His excellence to me, and I am content.
There's no better place to be than close to Him.
As we seek the Lord, we draw closer.
That's where He wants us, not afar.
We are called into His inner confines,
Where we can meet and commune with Him.
This is where we grow in depth.
We can increase in favour and maturity,
As we walk with Him.
There's no separation nor partition,

Because we are so close to His embrace.
We are one with the Lord in every way.
How great it is to grow in the fullness of Christ.
Only through intimate communion,
Can we become more like Him.
Cleansed and sanctified forever,
Behold a new creation.

Psalm 124

The Lord says-
"I have chosen you, my child.
Before creation, I knew you.
Your spirit lived in my heart.
I designed your life and ordained your days.
Though you were formless, I knew your shape.
I determined to create you for intimacy with me.
My heart longed to design you.
I set my mind on loving you and connecting you to me.
I desired that we be one,
That we would live together in my Garden.
I set out work for you and breathed my purpose on your life.
I know the plans for your growth.
I have sought to prosper you everywhere you go.
You are my chosen.
I will continually express my love for you.
I long to embrace you and to see your smile.
I desire to spend time with you,
You are mine.
I have called you to conquer with me.
I want you to reign with me,
To represent me across the lands and the oceans.

You will embark on great exploits for my name.
Nothing you go through will be in vain,
For everything will work towards your good.
I desire you.
I long that you desire me.
I want us to make a change together.
You are the apple of my eye.
Make me your first love.
You are my heir,
The possessor of my limitless treasure.
You have won the Lord's favour."

Psalm 125

He has called us to build.
He has called us to glorify His name.
We will build a monument of our Lord.
We will establish pillars of His glory in the nations.
We will witness miracles and wonders of His power.
We will add to the body of Christ.
We will make His name known.
For who will be able to deny the Lord,
When they see His glory pass by?
Who can withstand the heat of His presence,
When they gather to know His name?
We will build the body together
And tear down strongholds of evil.
He has called us to preach to the perishing,
And to rescue the fading ones.
He wants us to remember the vulnerable;
To make the poor man rich,
And the weak man strong.
We are to call those form darkness into the light,
To turn all defeats into victory.
That His name will be uttered in all the nations.
We shall labour until the time of His coming.

When He comes with His reward,
We will be expectant for Him to say,
That we built well.
That we ended up with more than we were given.

Psalm 126

The Lord has called us to a garden.
A place of peace and serenity.
He has allotted to us each a personal garden,
A place of private tranquillity.
It's in this refuge that we meet our Lord.
Filled with lush greenery and animals that speak,
His radiance sets the temperature,
And it puts us at ease.
We are ever so relaxed with Him.
It's a place we can access at any time,
We each have a unique key.
He permits us to decorate it as we like.
He wants it to reflect our passions and interests.
He makes things for our personal enjoyment.
We can find all these things in our personal retreat.
The air is perfect and easy to breathe.
There are angels who sing beautiful melodies.
Could there be a more a peaceful place than this?
The garden represents His presence of peace.
There are no burden or difficulties.
The garden holds everything we need.
Our Lord has fashioned it for us,

With our likes and interests to give us joy.
Step in whenever you feel and call to Him.
He will wait for you on the bench,
And point you to the springs.
The springs which carry the water of life.
They restore you from all the burdens you carry.
He wants you to rest in His embrace.
Go and run to the hills with Him in hand.
Watch the sunset from the green hills.
You will see the Man in white walking over to you.
From the horizon, radiating in pure white.

Psalm 127

The Lord is a shelter,
An umbrella to the vulnerable.
A place of safety and refuge,
From the rains of perils.
A large covering of peace,
From the scorching heat of anxieties.
A place of invisibility and hiding,
From the roaming lions and vipers.
His hand is very mighty,
And able to cover all His children.
He is a place of light,
Which illuminates every darkness.
The darkness cannot overcome it,
And it never will.
A safe shelter under which we can abide,
There could never be a safer place.
Through the prayers of the saints,
The umbrella becomes bigger,
As more gather to honour the protector.,
The manifest presence is more apparent.
The poor come to find richness in the Lord.
The lost come to be found in Him.

The ones in darkness seek the light,
The anxious man seeks peace of mind.
The Lord knows how to protect His people.
And even those who seek to be His own.
He will not permit His own to fall.
No, He has promised He will not lose any,
None.

Psalm 128

He has redeemed my life from the pit.
As He took His final breath,
I found my life.
The cross took my defeat,
That I may walk in victory.
He has shown me the way to life,
Through the mercy of His death.
I am reconciled and made a new.
As a servant of His glorious grace.
He has redeemed me from separation.
His cross has brought me to His God.
As I look upon the loving Son,
I am reminded that He cares for me.
Nothing can snatch me out of His hand.
Nothing can stand between me and my God.
He has redeemed me from all evil.
He is the reason for my life.
He has given me all I have.
He is the reason for who I am.
My life now belongs to Him.
The cross has purchased my life.
He says I belong to Him.
The cross reminds me of who has won:
The only beloved Son.

Psalm 129

"Christ is the end of the law,
For righteousness to everyone who believes."
He is the final atonement of all man.
Young, poor, old, rich,
Men from all cultural groups and tribes.
He is the final redemption.
He is the last answer.
The only solution to the saving grace of mankind.
There exists no alternative,
Nothing else but Christ who can pull,
All mankind and all flesh out of the fire.
He is the entirety of the law.
He is the perfect representation of fulfilment.
He is the purest sacrifice,
Carrying all righteousness and saving grace.
Able to save, He carries healing in His wings.
The perfect high priest who credits us with righteousness.
To present us holy and blameless,
Without stain nor filth,
Without blemish nor imperfection.
We are the redeemed and washed in His blood.
Believers are instantly justified as He enters their lives.

The only possible saving grace,
Who calls us to be accepted in the beloved.
To be perfected forever,
We are called.
We are now His possession,
A redeemed race.

Psalm 130

Lord I am under tension,
My spirit is being pressed.
No matter how much I cry,
I feel the pressure.
I feel the pain.
How much can I withstand?
I am drawn to You.
Your word is my only hope.
I only have You to seek.
Man cannot understand.
The sense of dread, it pains me.
Yet I have no fear,
For You, O Lord, have shown me,
The meaning of carrying my cross.
This is a call to endurance.
A call to purification,
You cause my flesh to be burned.
This is my service to You.
Though I want to run away,
You hold me in the pressing place to endure.
Though in pain, I can still stand firm.
The tension is strong, but it doesn't crush.

I call to You, Lord.
Please deliver me in Your compassion.
Make me strong,
Assemble people around me to encourage me.
I am never alone,
I abide in You.
You are my strong tower.
This pain leads to glory.
It is all counted toward greatness,
Thank you, Lord, for the victory.

Psalm 131

I keep my eyes on the prize.
That which God has promised,
Will surely come to pass.
Day by day I endure faithfully.
For he has promised goodness to me.
He has taught me to wait on Him.
He has made me quiet myself.
I am left with nothing but Him.
I cry out in my anguish, and He hears.
I wait patiently for the answer.
His spirit says "wait."
So, wait I shall on God.
His Word says to "be strong."
So, I am strengthened by His promises.
I need to endure.
I must press on to the upward call.
I must obtain the prize He has prepared.
I am matured and strengthened.
The tension lifts as I agree with Him.
Lord, I remain faithful to finish your work.
My calling is secured in the hands of God.
My perspective is fixed on overcoming challenges.

My muscles are trained.
My attitude is corrected.
I adjust my vision on seeking Him.
His Word carries me and washes me.
I am endowed with hope for the future.
He remains before me,
Answering all my prayers and petitions.
I praise Him because He always answers.
I am motivated to conquer,
It is my joy to persevere.

Psalm 132

Constant communion with Christ is the key to life.
We find our yes and hopes in Him.
For He is the firstborn over all the creation,
Therefore, He carries the ultimate inheritance.
For if we are to inherit all that God has prepared,
Then must come into communion with His bloodline.
The blood covenant of Christ wings us all things.
For the kingdom of heaven is ours to share.
Yes, He is our joy and peace.
He is our source of constant in many changes.
You have heard that He remains the same always.
His love prevails over all things.
Behold, the glory and lifter of our head.
Our previous Lord and saviour King,
Has forever won us every battle.
We yield to the victory of Christ.
We remain His to command.
How worthy is our great King,
Who carries us over the finish line.
He has called us to endure,
And to battle our hearts out for His name.
He leads us into every victory.

He is victorious forever and ever.
This is where communion is key.
We can defeat any stronghold of evil.
By God, we conquer all mountains.
Our crowns are given at each level.
We will remain strong under tension.
And endure till the end,
Relying on His communion.

Psalm 133

There is no darkness to the path He has called me to.
There is no fear in discovering the next step.
For He alone guides my step.
He predestines my every encounter.
Nothing is a surprise to Him.
He remains watchful over me.
I will not trip nor fall.
Even if I do, He raises me up quickly.
The Lord is compassionate towards me.
He sees my diligent pursuit.
He rewards me at each step,
Continuously encouraging me.
He builds me up at each challenge,
And works all things for my good.
He remains my constant companion,
The keeper of my soul.
He is the strength of my feet,
And He causes me to soar over mountains.
I have made Him my dwelling place,
Therefore, I am ever strengthened,
And my resolve is always renewed.
He is a source of unlimited power,

Which pushes me through each season.
I will magnify the name of my God.
He is most worthy of my praise.
I delight to do His will.
For He remains ever faithful to me.
He is my treasure and reward.
I remain in Him.

Psalm 134

I put on the Lord Jesus Christ.
He is the entirety of my armour.
He is my shield from my enemy's arrows.
He becomes my sword to do battle with;
The "Word became flesh" is my weapon.
He is my helmet when He gives me peace.
He covers my arms and legs when I run to conquer.
He covers me on all sides, even my blind spots.
For He sees what is to come.
Then He shares His strategies with me.
He gives me pointers to win,
The secret moves and methods to triumph.
He is my endurance to withstand strikes.
He covers my steps to I don't trip.
I can never lose now.
He sends His angels to go with me.
I have found a new strength.
My health is boosted for me.
His angels draw their swords of fire,
And vanquish the remaining foes.
My enemies scatter in their shame,
As they cannot face the living God.

They have carved their own imaginations into store.
How vain to pray to the blind and deaf!
My God hears my cry for help.
He speaks me to my victory.

Psalm 135

James speaks of remaining steadfast.
Despite the winds and the waves,
We are called to remain firm in our conviction.
Let not our feet be moved from the ground,
Let not our face be turned away from our conviction.
We hope in the Lord alone.
Let us dig deep as we are tested.
No one can escape the testing.
As we move forward in God,
Our testing increases.
All our faith is counted and observed,
By the One who sees everything.
Let steadfastness be worked out in you,
You who hope in the Lord.
Wait patiently and suffer well.
He defines your character through struggles.
He moulds us according to His pleasure.
He knows what He is doing.
The Lord richly rewards them,
Those whose feet are planted firmly.
Thoe who are not carried away by the wind.
Those whose homes do not crumble.

They are favoured and advance further.
He has crowns to adorn them with.
Various trials may meet the believer,
But the Lord promises peace.
"My peace I give to you, not as the world giveth."
He determines to walk the believer through the storms,
To the other side of growth and victory.
You will win.

Psalm 136

Where do our gifts come from?
The Father of lights.
Where do we receive our joy and gladness?
The Father of lights.
Who replaces our pain with His goodness?
The Father of lights.
Where do our answered prayers come from?
The Father of lights.
He alone gives us all that is good.
He will not withhold a good thing.
Our joy will be made complete.
As we smile and leap for joy,
So does the Father upon His throne.
He works in us according to His pleasure,
As He intends good for us each day.
We can expect good things to overtake us.
The Lord works goodness out of pain.
Joy out of misery.
Beauty out of rain.
Flowers out of thorns.
Redemption out of evil.
Mercy out of wickedness.

Confidence out of shame.
Character out of pain.
These things the Lord has intended for us.
Goodness follows us daily.
Our eyes must remain open.
To see each unwrapped present,
Falling into our laps.

Psalm 137

The Lord hears the prayers of His own.
He inclines His ears towards His righteous.
Those who are His pray with conviction.
The Lord's ears are open to their cries.
He moves upon the faith of the saints.
His angels carry the prayer of His saints.
They go up through the firmament,
Towards the golden gates of heaven.
They find their way to the bowls at His altar,
And are presented before the throne of God.
The faithful One judges justly.
He observes the requests of His saints,
And He begins to answer.
The Lord works behind the scenes,
Or He openly answers.
Regardless, the Lord hears everything.
He seeks deeper faith on the earth.
The prayer of faith moves His hand greatly.
God is pleased with His people.
He promises that the prayers of His saints will be effective.
Prayer warriors are raised up for this task;
To pray the manifestation of God's will.

That the earth may see the Lord's face,
His mighty hand at work in the lives of the downcast.
The world must see that God sees all.
He hears all.
He knows all.
He moves to answer prayer.
He will act.
So, pray continually.

Psalm 138

Those who believe are ever evolving.
We are being translated from glory to glory.
When we have experienced all growth in one platform,
His mighty hand carries us up to the next one.
We are required to seek God all over again,
As a new level requires a different approach,
It holds a different challenge.
We are always seeking Him, and it never ends.
Our perspectives change,
So does our faith.
We develop new tools in prayer and worship.
We see things differently and develop more of the Lord's nature.
Habits are changed as strongholds are broken.
Endurance and resilience go hand in hand with the increase,
And so does our love for the Lord.
The spirit realm is opened in a grander scale as He reveals more of His glory.
We engage with Him in high authorities and are given greater assignments.
We must press on to the higher call in Christ,
To access the greater unseen things, He has called us into.
The mysteries of the kingdom are for us to discover.
What is unseen is far more than we can comprehend.
There is more of the unseen than the seen.
The secrets are endless, and He calls us into an eternal discovery.

Psalm 139

I bless the Lord.
I bless His name continually.
I remember His faithfulness and good works to me.
I know that He works for my benefit.
I seek Him continually.
He rewards and continually blesses me.
He sees me where I am.
He does not waste my life.
He carries me forward.
I rest in Him.
No matter the situation, I know how to see Him working.
I know how to spot Him in every detail.
For He is always present with me.
He has promised to never leave me.
He continues His faithfulness to me.
When I want to run away, He brings me back to Himself.
His love always coaxes me.
Where would I go to?
There's nowhere sweeter than His presence.
I have tasted of His goodness.
I have lived in His will.
I cannot go anywhere else.
Nothing else would satisfy me.
I would drown without Him.

Psalm 140

You have heard it said, "deep calls unto deep."
The Lord is eternal.
There are endless depths in Him.
There is never an end to discovering Him.
Step by step we see more.
Ever increasingly are we exposed to a different aspect of Him.
We behold His endless beauty and character.
We can never become too familiar with Him.
The seeking of God is an eternal venture.
Who can arrive at its end,
When He has no end?
Each day there is something new to discover.
He has new revelations in store.
He shares newer secrets as we pursue.
The road is never ending.
Though you may reach what seems to be the end of a journey,
He is only preparing the new road for you to embark on.
The waters of His love and mercy are so deep.
Yet He desires us to go deeper in Him.
When we look back, we should see that we have come so far.
He is too good to resist.
We must consume more of Him.
His Word is an everlasting life source.

Psalm 141

Consider those who walked before us,
How they presented themselves as faithful before His sight.
In faith, they committed themselves to Him,
As to a faithful creator.
They served Him very well.
Their endurance and patience inherited favour.
Moreover, they left an example for the rest of the brethren,
And for the future generations of those who would inherit Jesus as Lord.
No one would die for a lie.
No one would be hunted for a fable.
Jesus became their reality.
Yahweh became their truth.
With conviction of the truth, they suffered.
Glady.
Ever holding onto their faith.
Abraham believed God and left everything behind.
God was worth the discomfort and the unknown.
Moses suffered with his people,
Rather than enjoying the riches of a false kingdom.
Noah endured mockery but worked to build.
He knew was to come despite what he saw or heard.

Sarah knew the faithfulness of God personally,
As she contended with facing the impossible.
The apostles of Christ preached their hearts out,
Despite persecution.
How could they deny the Risen Christ?
He was all they saw and became like Him.
We look at the early church in Rome,
How they faced lions in the games and were burnt alive in the street.
Their bodies hung as a display.
They dared to oppose the emperor as the false god of the day,
Reckoning Jesus as Lord over his rule.
Did they die for a false prophet?
Paul endured chains continually but persevered.
He looked to Christ who remained by His side,
Turning him left, guiding him right,
But ever faithful,
Whispering hope into the Roman's ear.
Should we fail and fall?
Or should we study their examples of endurance and strive for the upward call?
Not all of us have suffered bloodshed.
We must look to the reward.
"The Name of the Lord is a strong tower,
The righteous man runs into it and is safe."
How fleeting is our life, even the pain we suffer.

But He promises eternal satisfaction,
For the faithful ones who endure to the end.
For those who carry His name.
Suffer now,
But reap glory forever.
In the world to come,

Sharing the same seat of Christ Jesus.

Psalm 142

Cast your cares upon Him,
Deliberately throw upon Him what concerns you.
Sound off and make it known to Him;
The troubles which ail you,
For He cares for you.
He keeps His watchful eye trained upon you.
The created beings are known to God.
He remembers even the minute details of your life.
He considers the most fleeting thoughts that you have.
His recollection of what matters to you is vast.
Is there anyone like Him who can catch your tears and keep them in
His jar?
He can sympathise and feel what you feel.
He carries your burdens and fights your battles.
He watches over your surroundings when you sleep.
"His Angel encamps those who fear Him,
And He sends His angel to deliver them."
He appoints salvation to the believer,
And provides him with the hope of an eternal inheritance,
Which is imperishable forever.
He cares for His children's life on the earth and beyond.
He desires to hear the hearts cries of His children.

He promises to them out of all trouble.
"He knows how to rescue the godly".
The righteous cry out and the Lord will always care enough to save them.

Psalm 143

Yod Heh Waw Heh as known by your servant Moses.
Adonai is My Lord and Master. Gladly I serve Him.
El Shaddai the Almighty One, nothing can match Him.
Elohim is the creator of all things seen and unseen, intricate designer.
Nissi is the flag of my victory which I uphold in battle and adversity.
El Roi sees me no matter what is happening. I am never unseen.
Yireh will "supply all my needs according to His riches in glory in Christ."
Shammah will always show up, and we will declare He remains "there".
Yahweh Raah leads me. His Shepherd's rod and staff; they give me comfort.
Yahweh Shalom is the Prince of Peace. Your peace you leave with me, not as the world giveth.
Yahweh Rophe has healed all my diseases. He has made me whole by His wounds.

Psalm 144

The flowers bloom when the Lord walks by.
They grow for you and I.
They come to life by His neuma.
They twirl and shine with bright colours.
They adorn the field with beauty.
The Lord walks and brings them for you and me.
Good gifts He brings for His children.
Gifts of life and not of harm.
Each flower has its beautiful dance.
A performance of love and sweet charm,
A synchronised twirl amongst the others,
For the Lord when He walks by.
He prunes them that they may exemplify His beauty.
He speaks to them that they may know who they are.
They speak back to Him praising His name.
They are named individually by Him.
He knows the form of each petal and vine.
Each seed planted by His hand,
He has chosen them to be filled with beauty.
They are grown for you and me.
He picks them and arrays them in a bouquet,
To present to us as a reminder of His kisses.

"But if God so clothes the grass of the field, which today is alive and tomorrow is thrown into the oven, will he not much more clothe you, O you of little faith?" - Matthew 6:30

Psalm 145

In the morning or the evening,
He bids me to come.
To go for a walk with Him in nature,
To feel the gentle breeze.
Whether in rain or in the sunshine,
I am motivated because I get to find Him.
I get to know Him more.
I get to experience Him in my prayer walks.
He speaks hope to me.
I lose track of my surroundings with each step forward,
As I begin to hear more of His voice.
The voice of the Lord overtakes every sound.
It a sweet, sweet sound which speaks to body, soul and spirit.
I forget that I am walking,
And I feel that I am floating.
I am so fixed on the future,
Which He describes as hopeful and joyful.
He speaks and reveals.
Prophetic insight is all I hear.
He promises to fulfill all my dreams and wishes,
As I keep Him first and foremost.
He is my ultimate delight.

I cross the pathways,
Across the roads,
Over the bridges,
Through the bushes,
Under the trees,
Amongst all His creation.
The birds sing to me.
I feel Him walking with me.
I pray at each step and am met
with love.
I can feel His good pleasure and
acceptance in my bones.
His shalom peace covering me.
My prayer walks bring us closer together.
Intimacy with the Son of God.
Our relationship is built.
I have not known such perfect peace,
Such immeasurable joy.
I am convinced that there is much hope,
And contentment in His presence.
I will keep walking,
And keep praying.
I will continue to seek that I may find.
He Spirit will carry me,
And continue to speak hope and salvation to me.

Psalm 146

The warrior is positioned for his
battle.
With his shield raised and
sword drawn.
He utters boldly,
"Blessed be the Lord my God,
He trains my hands for warfare.
He prepares my fingers to do
battle."
Scattered amongst his foes,
The warrior readies himself.
He fears no death.
Ever ready for combat.
The eyes of the wicked burn with hatred when they see him.
The warrior of light cladded with the Armor of God.
The ungodly surround him and hurl curses and threats.
He smirks for their time is short.
They taunt him and mock his God.
"Can his God save him now?
Or shall we destroy him?"
The warrior is intimately acquainted with the peace and joy of his
salvation.

He has nothing to lose, but everything to gain.
He entrusts His soul to the faithful creator, as scripture instructs.
He remains steadfast.
Having done all to remain firm, he stands.
He has been tested and refined through trials and trainings,
He is conditioned for war.
He does not fear death,
And he shall not see it.
He will live forever.
The battlefield becomes silent as the enemy prepares to charge.
They lunge forward and run, coming from all sides.
Like a cohort of horses, they trample the ground,
Charging headfirst towards the warrior.
He remains grounded.
A war cry thunders from the heavens.
His God has been keeping a watchful eye.
The Angel of the Lord rapidly descends.
Tearing open the sky like lighting,
And flying through his enemies at the speed of light.
The warrior laughs and follows forth.
He charges in after the Angel.
He finishes the stragglers and mops up the remains.
The Angel has left a devastation in its wake.
The ground is littered with lighting strikes and burning.
Today, the Lord has fought for his faithful warrior.

He sent his Angel forth to go before him and deliver him from his enemies.
The warrior raises a banner to the Lord and proclaims the land as His.
The righteous will win every battle,
And overcome any form of adversaries.
Their God is always watching.

Psalm 147

Called to forget,
The former things of old.
We a see a new thing coming.
A new spring arising,
From the dry and barren ground.
With fresh revelation and strength.
A new hope with motivation.
Called to forget,
What holds us back.
We keep our eyes on Him.
He shows us new things,
To keep us strong.
We are ever progressing.
Our futures are set in Him,
Firm as stone.
So why look back?
Time only moves forward.
Can you not see?
The new is coming and the old is fading.
He ordains our steps, forward.
He is raising up destinies.
He is ordaining victories.

Covenant futures are born.
He is redeeming the time.
The future is bright,
Covered with radiant glory.
A new hope and future,
Prepared for us to walk in.
A great arising is taking place,
An advancement of His army.
Nothing can stop it.
He knows the plans He has for us.
Plans for us to reign in Him,
For this life and the next.
"Our times are in His hand."
He conceives victory,
Our hopeful destinies.

Psalm 148

The Story of the Servant

The servant is at the end of his life.
He has a lived one of sacrifice.
He carried his cross all his days,
And his time is coming to an end.
He is being poured out as a drink offering,
Upon the altar of his God.
Laying on his bed, he reflects on his years on the earth.
Selah.

O, how they have been filled with trials and grieving,
Yet strength and overcoming.
He had been brought to new levels of conquering,
Being translated from glory to glory.
But required to endure hardship and pain,
To grow in his capacity.
To carry greater measures of God's presence in him,
As he travelled the nations proclaiming the message of repentance.
Selah.

O, he was given all his heart's desires.
The King did not withhold any good thing from him.
The servant kept his eyes on the Lord throughout.

And he welcomed each good and perfect gift with thanksgiving and praise.
Remaining humble and knowing that God is the one "who giveth and taketh away."
Always blessing the name of the Lord.
Selah.

There were many times he fell short,
Often giving into the flesh,
But trying to walk in step with the spirit.
He gave his weaknesses to his God,
And found himself becoming stronger,
Overcoming the flesh and walking in constant sanctification.
He remembered the faithfulness of God,
Who was always willing to forgive the servant based upon his short accounts and confessions.
Selah.

From his younger years till his older days,
Until his hair was white,
The Lord stood by Him and strengthened him as promised.
He remained his God until the servant's hair was white.
He constantly showed up and delivered the righteous man from his troubles:
All the troubles.
Selah.

The man had every possession,
But it was all empty to him.
He grasped how Solomon felt.
He knew that life was more than food, wealth and honour.
It was about living off the daily Word of God.
Both written and spoken.
It was about intimacy and fellowship with Jesus,
Which satisfied him.
Nothing in the earth could satisfy him.
He needed to seek God all over again in the morning when he woke,
Dispute being full of joy from the night before.
God's beautiful way of drawing his servant to Himself each day.
Selah.

At the end of his life,
He gets ready to depart.
For he knew he has left a legacy and an example of serving God.
He had shown the next generation how to follow the living God.
How to hear His voice,
And how to minister to the person of Jesus.
He taught how to make disciples,
Raise churches,
But also, how to endure and to suffer well.
How to let God kill the flesh.
He taught others how to bear their cross and walk through the
straight and narrow.

He taught them all that God required,
Fulfilling his personal Great Commission.
Selah.

As he lays down and shuts his eyes,
Surrounded by family and friends.
He utters his final words and takes his last few breaths.
He begins to hear the angels singing in the distant.
The sounds of sobs of his loved ones begin to decrease,
As the voice of the angels grow,
Extending their welcomes to him.
He can't see them, but he can hear them.
Though it is the middle of winter,
The room has a soft warmth.
Which grows slowly, it is tangible and he is comforted.
The ceiling is filled with light and a portal opens.
His gaze is caught by the familiar faces he sees in the portal.
All dressed in white are the friends of old,
And the people he ministered to on the earth.
Clothed in brightness.
He is covered in peace but perplexed.
What a pleasant surprise.
Selah, God is good.

He drifts away slowly,
With his hands held by his loved ones.

Every sound is drowned out and he stops breathing.
He awakes quickly at the 'point of death'
His eyes shoot open, he is seated.
Behold, stands a Man in white,
Admiring the servant with great pleasure.
The angels begin to sing loudly and hum pleasantly.
The One of whom he preached all his life,
Stands before Him.
The Holy One of Israel has come before him.
Adorned in beauty, with the servant's rewards in His hand.

The Lord has come to receive His spirit,
To bring the man into peace and tranquillity,
To a kingdom out of time and space.
He is called home, forever.

Psalm 149

The Prayer of Purpose

Lord Jesus,
I am ready to be brought in,
To accomplish my ultimate destiny.
I let go of every distraction,
Every false weight,
Every wrong purpose and my pride.
I pick up my cross and say:
"I am ready."
I am ready to live for the kingdom purpose.
I no longer live,
But Christ abides in me.
You are my strength,
And my joy is to do your will.
I forsake all else,
I strive forward to the goal for your prize,
Which is in the upward call of God on my life.
I will seek you each day,
Within the confines of your new mercies.
I will mediate on your faithfulness,
And be encouraged by your overwhelming love.
I will soak in your presence,

And be set apart unto your holiness.
Hand in hand we walk, Lord.
I am ready for my final calling.
I ask that you fulfill all righteousness in my life.
Keep my eyes on what's coming.
Show me the treasures of your kingdom.
I live for You.
I will live well on the earth to finish my ministry.
My heart is where You are.
I live for the world to come.
Forever eternal life.
Amen.

Psalm 150

The end of all things

How far are willing to be obedient?
The Son was led to the slaughter, remaining silent.
Keeping us in mind through the pain and suffering.
For the joy set before His eyes.
Will we keep our God in mind during pain and suffering?
The Lord Christ destroyed His body and bled for our lives.
Could we not shed a little blood nor suffer for His Name's sake?
What is there to hold onto, besides Him alone.
All else is so temporary.
There is nothing glorious this can offer.
Would we reject Him to save ourselves?
Or would we remain silent and endure?
He will be with us in gruesome persecution.
We ought to confess His name through pain.
We will not object, nor will we curse our persecutors.
Gladly we suffer,
Gladly we hold onto Him.
As each stone strikes our body,
As each strike of the whip tears our backs open,
One more portion of heaven opens to us in the clouds.
Behold, we see the Son of Man sitting on the clouds of glory.

He comes with fire and thunder in His breath.
The True Judge is the witness to our persecution.
He waits.
With each strike to our foreheads,
With each drop of our blood,
We see the angels around us, preparing to raise us to the clouds
We see the Son of God with arms wide open ready to receive us.
Are we prepared to depart in glory?
Or will we hold onto the world and temporary possessions.
Will we reject Him after all this pain?
Jesus is amongst the crowd of those who curse and taunt.
Look! Can you see the white amongst the black?
He waits patiently for your final breath,
Beckoning you forward.
You see Him and He strengthens you
The peace of God overflows your heart.
You forget all the pain.

Finish your race.
Before the final blow of the rod,
By merely a second,
He snatches your spirit out of your body.
You do not experience the point of death,
You are raised into heaven.
You soar through the clouds with the cohort of angels.

Oh, how they rejoice over you.
Faster than the speed of light, you ascend.
You can smell the fresh aroma of perfection and all that is holy.
You don't look back at the world nor the filth,
You've already forgotten it.
Your smile gets bigger, and bigger.
The Lord Christ places You on His chariot.
And you ride off into glory with Him forever,
To be amongst the company of prophets, saints, angels, all beings; unseen.
Forever abiding in the safety of Father's arms.
Fully rewarded and highly situated in the honour of heaven's realms.
Your head bears the crowns of eternity.

Glory is perfect.
Now and forever, Jesus and you.
World without end.
Amen.

"And if I go and prepare a place for you, I will come back and take you to be with me that you also may be where I am."
-a promise of Jesus in John 14:3
When you see the end of all things, all your priorities change.
Thank you, Lord Jesus.

Precious Lord,

I have completed the work that you have set before me.

I have prayed before writing and written what I have heard from You.

Lord, I pray that as each person has read this book until the end, the Word of God would ruminate in their hearts and that they would walk away with a fresh idea of who Christ is.

This work is not about myself, but about bringing Jesus to life in the hearts of many.

My prayer is that this book would reach the nations and touch the lives of many.

I pray many hearts would be changed and turn to You.

Thank You for the privilege of working for You to bring this project to life.

I look forward to Your coming.

Amen.

Keshan Singh

www.ingramcontent.com/pod-product-compliance
Lightning Source LLC
LaVergne TN
LVHW091048080826
845145LV00002B/662

* 9 7 8 1 7 6 4 5 6 2 0 4 1 *